Haunted Travels of Michigan III

SPIRITS RISING

T0206703

Kathleen Tedsen & Beverlee Rydel

Holt, Michigan

OF MICHIGAN

Haunted Travels of Michigan, Volume III: Spirits Rising
by Kathleen Tedsen & Beverlee Rydel

Published by
Thunder Bay Press
Holt, Michigan 48842

First Printing July 2013
16   15   14   13   1   2   3   4   5

ISBN: 978-1-933272-41-2
Library of Congress Control Number: 2013943400

Book, cover, and maps design by Julie Taylor.
Front and back cover photo: Beverlee Rydel and Kathleen Tedsen.

Printed in the United States of America

Dedicated to the memory of

Christian E. Tedsen

A universal truth. Everything ends like the final chapter of a great book. We close the book. It's over. The people we've loved, cherished, are a chapter in our life. We must one day say goodbye. The pain seems insurmountable, but in our pain we know they will remain a part of us. Our solid ground. Our Northstar.

You will always remain our Northstar.

Story Locations

Contents

Acknowledgements

We want to thank the many people who helped us with this book.

We are especially grateful to the owners/managers for allowing us to investigate their property and sharing information.

Someone we certainly cannot forget is James Sturgill. Jim provided editorial assistance with many of our stories, before going to the publisher.

We are especially thankful for the investigators and paranormal teams we had the pleasure of working with as well as the knowledgeable historians who helped to fill in some of the blanks.

Our "Special Thanks" to the following:

EDITORIAL ASSISTANCE
James Sturgill

INVESTIGATORS AND PARANORMAL TEAMS
Maria Holt-Aistrop
Donald Altman
Todd Clements, Haunts of Mackinac
Lynn Donaldson
Robert and Shari Dowd, C.H.I.P.S. (Clarkston Haunted
    Investigative Paranormal Seekers/Supernatural)
Dawn James
Melanie Land (Moyer) and Matt Moyer, Mid-Michigan
    Paranormal Investigators
Jenny Marcus and Lisa Mann, Highland Ghost Hunters
Tammy Schuster, Psychic/Medium

HISTORIANS
Tara Chapko
Sandy Stamm

Story Secret Rooms

How to Use Our Interactive Web site
www.HauntedTravelsMI.com

To help bring you into each story, we have established a Web site, www.HauntedTravelsMI.com, with a "Secret Room" for each story. This Secret Room will include audio, video, and full color photographic evidence. It will also have some behind-the-scene video clips and/or photographs of what happened during the investigation.

Secret Rooms are Password Protected

Each story has a secret password that will unlock the room. You must enter a separate password for each Secret Room.

High Speed Internet Recommended

Because the file size for some videos, photos, and audio clips are large, for best results, you should have a broadband or high speed Internet connection. You can use dial-up, but you'll need patience.

How It Works

Step One: Go to our Web site: www.HauntedTravelsMI.com and click on "Secret Rooms." This will get you to the doorway to enter the Main Secret Room Vault. You'll see a wooden door. *CLICK ON THE DOOR HANDLE.*

Step Two: You are now in the Main Secret Room. Click on the number associated with the story, (example: Bath School Disaster is Story 1).

Step Three: Once you click on the number, a dialogue box will come up saying you're about to enter a password protected page. *CLICK OK.*

```
[JavaScript Application]

THIS SITE IS PASSWORD PROTECTED, DO YOU STILL WANT
TO ENTER?

                              ( Cancel )   ( OK )
```

Step Four: The Password box will come up. Carefully *ENTER THE PASSWORD* from the story, then *CLICK OK.*

```
WHAT IS THE PASSWORD?

|

                              ( Cancel )   ( OK )
```

Step Five: Another dialogue box will come up. If you've entered the password correctly, it will let you know. *CLICK OK.* If you've entered the wrong password, it will re-direct you back to our main page. You'll need to try again.

```
http://www.mivg.com
CORRECT! CLICK OK.

                                      ( OK )
```

That's it!
You've unlocked the Story Secret Room door.
Your virtual experience begins.

Story One:
Bath School Disaster

Bath, Michigan
Guest Investigator: Maria Holt-Aistrop

Password: bsdk313

Andrew Kehoe, The Mad Murderer of Bath

THE MAD MURDERER OF BATH, that's what people of Bath called Andrew Kehoe. The demented man, on May 18, 1927, bombed the Bath Consolidated School. His hatred and violent insanity resulted in the death of thirty-eight children and seven adults along with an estimated fifty-eight injuries. This horrific disaster eclipses even the profoundly tragic Sandy Hook and Columbine school massacres. The story is ugly. It's difficult to understand what caused that man's mind to twist into such unthinkable decay.

For many years there have been reports of paranormal activity at the site where the school once stood and at Pleasant Hill Cemetery, where some of the victims are interred. It is said that the sound of children crying or the light touch from small unseen hands is not an uncommon occurrence. In the cemetery, ghostly shadows have been seen moving across the quiet grounds.

Are these locations truly *haunted* or is it simply the expectations and imaginations of over zealous people believing a tragedy of this scope would leave its mark? That is what our investigations hoped to discover.

We must say that from the beginning, this is one of those investigations that troubled both of us. In fact, whether or not we should go forward with it was discussed at some length. When it was finally decided, our intent was to approach it showing the greatest respect for the lives of those lost on that profoundly tragic day. May 18, 1927, should never be forgotten.

This story and our subsequent investigations deal with a difficult subject matter and may not be appropriate for all ages.

Although much has been written about events of that fateful spring day, little has been said about Andrew Kehoe. Perhaps they believed this evil man called the *Mad Murderer of Bath* should be forgotten. They believe he does not deserve to be remembered. But to understand what happened, we need to understand Andrew Kehoe. Who was he and what caused his mind to step into twisted darkness?

Our research began. Bev and I dug through massive files of newspaper clippings, death records, journals, inquest transcripts, and books. One book in particular was quite revealing. It was written by Arnie Bernstein, *Bath Massacre: America's First School Bombing*. Over a period of months, we put the pieces of the story together.

February 1, 1872, in Tecumseh, Michigan, Andrew Kehoe was born. He was the first-born son of Philip Kehoe and Mary McGovern and would be raised in a large family.

Andrew's fascination with electricity started at a very young age. While other children were outside playing, he would remain secluded in his father's barn developing and testing electrically powered equipment and gadgets. Of course, in those very early days, his experiments were rudimentary and not very practical, but his interest in electricity grew.

Philip, Andrew's father, was a dominant figure in the household with a strong personality. Much of his days were spent working the farm. Philip also served in several elected political roles. This took up a good part of his days leaving little time for his family. As was common back then, the wife took control of raising the children. For Andrew's mother, Mary, it was a difficult role.

Mary was stricken with a painful disorder that affected her nervous system. By the time Andrew was ten years old, his mother's illness kept her in bed a good deal of the time. When he turned eighteen, she was in full paralysis. Her painful decline was difficult for the children to witness. All they could do was watch as it progressed. Mary mercifully succumbed to her condition November 5, 1890.

At the time of Mary's death, Andrew's father, Philip, was sixty years old and afflicted with both arthritis and the early stages of Parkinson's disease. In spite of—or perhaps because of—his own worsening condition, he quickly remarried. Her name was Frances Wilder, a widow younger than Philip by twenty-eight years with children of her own.

There was an instant dislike between Andrew and Frances. In fact, it's said they detested each other. Andrew left home. He attended Michigan State College (now Michigan State University) and took several electrical engineering courses. Andrew eventually headed west to St. Louis, Missouri, where he completed additional studies in electrical engineering.

While in Missouri, Andrew had an accident. Exactly what happened is unclear. He either received a massive jolt of electricity or fell from a ladder. Andrew could not remember much of the accident. It left him in a coma for two weeks. Some believe Andrew's injury muddled his brain.

In the years that followed, Andrew drifted around the Midwest. Nearing the age of forty, he returned to his father's home and quickly discovered much had changed in his absence.

Philip's arthritis and advancing Parkinson's disease had crippled this once strong, dominant man. He needed the support of a cane to get around and, even then, his movements were painful, slow, and lumbering. His father now depended heavily on Frances' care. Adding to the household changes was Philip and Frances' three year old daughter, Irene. There was a new child in the family, and Andrew wasn't especially happy about that.

Andrew's resentment of Frances grew. Perhaps one reason was that, as the eldest son, he was expected to inherit his father's estate. However, Philip's *new* family placed his inheritance in jeopardy.

Not wanting to be around Frances, Andrew spent a good deal of time away from the home working the farm and tinkering with equipment. One of the things he enjoyed most was clearing fields, which required blowing up tree stumps, boulders, and other blockages to the land. His fascination and knowledge of electricity merged perfectly with rigging explosive devices.

It was around lunch time on Sunday, September 17, 1911, when Frances came into the kitchen to prepare something to eat. The stove was either a gasoline or oil-burning stove, exactly which is unclear. In any event, it had a pilot that needed to be manually lit.

Frances bent forward with the burning match in her hand. As she approached the pilot, the stove exploded. Flames and petroleum shot out, covering her head and upper body in searing heat. It was so sudden, so unexpected, for a brief moment the poor woman was unaware the fire surrounded her. Then the pain hit, immense, powerful, overwhelming. She began to scream.

Her body mindlessly circled the room bumping against anything in her way. Inflamed arms frantically and uselessly pounded at the fire that now consumed her head and rapidly ignited her clothing as it traveled down her body. According to reports, the intensity of the heat was so extreme the water and blood of her body virtually boiled the flesh.

Both Philip and Andrew were at home. They heard the explosion and screams. Crippled, Philip was slow to respond but Andrew quickly arrived. He saw a pitcher of water and threw it on her. Of course, using water to dowse a flame ignited by gasoline or oil is the worst thing you can do. It thins the petroleum and spreads the fire faster.

Eventually the flames were extinguished. Frances was ruined, nearly unrecognizable yet still alive, completely aware, and in immense pain. Together Philip and Andrew managed to get her in bed. When the doctor finally arrived, there was not much he could do. She remained conscious and in agony for some time before slipping into a coma. Her death record states she passed at 5:00 a.m. the next morning.

Frances' death was considered an accident. Was it? To this day some wonder if Andrew *tinkered* with the stove to cause the unexpected blast. It is one of the many questions that will never be answered.

One thing was certain. With Frances gone the farm would be Andrew's after his father's death. He did not have to wait long. Four years later his father died from the affects of Parkinson's disease. The land belonged to Andrew Kehoe.

Not long after Frances' tragic death, Andrew decided a change in his life was needed. He re-established a friendship with a former girlfriend, Ellen Price. Friends and family called her Nellie. The two were married just four months later.

Nellie Kehoe

Nellie came from a well off family. Her Uncle Laurence was a very successful automotive businessman in the Lansing area and a prominent politician. He owned a good-sized plot of farmland in Bath. With his responsibilities in Lansing keeping him very busy, Nellie's father stepped in to run the farming operation.

When Uncle Laurence died, Andrew negotiated a deal with the family to buy the farm. A price was agreed upon. Andrew sold his father's farm and the couple moved in to Nellie's family home in Bath, Michigan.

Andrew and Nellie Kehoe's farmhouse in Bath, Michigan

From what we've read, we can't say the neighbors disliked Andrew Kehoe although they did think he was a little strange. He'd often be seen plowing the fields in a suit coat and crisp white shirt. In fact, he was meticulously clean, changing his shirt or clothing the minute they became soiled.

He was also known to be impatient, demonstrating a sharp anger when people disagreed with him. Although he was always there to help his neighbors, if they crossed him, he would quickly retaliate with strong verbal assaults. Many of his farm animals suffered much harsher abuse. He exhibited unusual cruelty toward the animals and was said to have beaten at least one of his horses to death.

Andrew's interest and skills were clearly not in farming. He spent more time tinkering with farm equipment than managing the crops. As a result, his farm did not prosper and his funds were quickly depleted.

To make matters worse, Nellie had become quite ill. According to a popular genealogy web site, she had contracted tuberculosis. At the time, there were no antibiotics and no cure for the disease. Her illness required extended hospital stays which meant additional costs Andrew could not afford.

In 1924, Andrew was elected to serve as School Board Treasurer. The next year, after the death of a township board member, Andrew was appointed township clerk. Also, because of his strong mechanical and electrical abilities, he was asked to serve as the maintenance man for the Bath school. He agreed and was given a key allowing him access to the building at any time of the day or night. His presence on the board and in the community gave Andrew a certain sense of importance, and he seemed relatively happy.

Unfortunately, heated arguments with board members and community leaders did not sit well with the others. At one point, he accused the well-liked school superintendent, Emory Huyck, of financial mismanagement. In 1926 Andrew Kehoe lost the election.

That is when things changed. Andrew's life and mind began to crumble. Nellie's illness required more extended hospital stays. Money grew tighter.

Adding to Andrew's woes, the community wanted to build a new consolidated school. This would require a significant increase in property taxes to pay for its construction. Andrew was strongly against it and fought against the tax increase. He was enraged when the community voted for it and the bill passed.

Andrew's life seemed hopeless, and he blamed everyone but himself for his troubles. People had defied his wishes and passed this ridiculous tax increase. He would not tolerate it!

Andrew stopped paying property taxes and making mortgage payments. He refused to negotiate agreements with his creditors.

The mortgage lender threatened foreclosure. He shrugged it off and let his farm go to seed. Nothing was working for him. Nothing. 1926 was a defining year for Andrew Kehoe. That's when his plot for revenge began.

Bath School, before the bombing.

It was a beautiful, sunny morning in Bath, Michigan, May 18, 1927. The end of the school year was nearing. The children were unusually excited, eager to begin their summer vacations.

Bernice Sterling, first grade teacher at the Bath school tried to settle her students down. To help work off their pent-up energy, she put them though a marching exercise.

It was about 9:45 a.m. and, as directed by Bernice, the children dutifully marched around the classroom. Suddenly a massive sound rocked the room. Bernice would later compare the feeling to a huge earthquake.

Ms. Sterling, in an article taken from the Trenton Evening Times, May 19, 1927, tells her story:

> *"It seemed as if the floor went up several feet. After the first shock, I thought for a moment I was blind. When it came, the air seemed to be full of children and flying desks and books. Children were tossed high in the air; some were catapulted out of the building.*
>
> *Children were hurled through windows and over crumbling walls to light in the school yard, dead."*

North wing of the school destroyed.

Not long after the bombing, in 1927, Monty J. Ellsworth wrote an account of that day in a self-published book called *The Bath School Disaster*. One of the chapters was written by fifteen-year old, Martha Hintz, who recounts her memories.

Martha was in the assembly hall with other students. Superintendent Huyck and a teacher, Mr. Flory, were giving final examinations. Without warning a massive crash and explosion was heard and felt. So powerful, it violently shook the entire room. Plaster from the walls and ceilings began to rain down on them as children were violently tossed from their seats.

Screams and panic began almost immediately. Some ran wildly for the charred and bent door while others made their way to windows. The superintendent calmed the children down and called them to order. Eventually each was safely helped out of windows. Superintendant Huyck remained behind until everyone was gone.

Once on the ground, Martha was ecstatic to see her brother was safe. For several moments they held each other tightly. The next thing she recalled was seeing the mass of people coming. They came from every direction, running frantically on foot or driving a variety of machines. All converged at the now ruined school, its entire north side gone.

Without the need for words, men and women immediately joined and began clearing away the wreckage, pulling out children one after the other. Their little faces and bodies were bleeding and horribly torn. Some cried in fear and pain, others only whimpered, while others didn't utter a sound or move at all. For fifteen-year-old Martha, it was the most dreadful vision she had ever seen.

Eventually one of the teachers gathered Martha and some of her classmates together. Their small group carefully made their way to the front of the building just as another massive blast occurred. They thought it was the school again, but it wasn't. It had come from outside. They had no idea what was going on and turned, running from the explosions and horrible vision of crying, torn, bleeding, or dead children. They continued running until they were at an oil station some distance away.

It was then Martha turned to see a massive fire in the western sky. They had no idea what it could be. Not long after, the sound of rescue came. Alarms and sirens filled the air as a line of cars and ambulances sped down the street toward Bath and the school. People cheered as the rescuers approached.

Doctors, nurses and medical aides from surrounding areas converged and took control. Bodies were laid on the grassy schoolyard forming long lines. Each lifeless form covered with whatever blankets or sheets could be found.

Frenzied parents desperately searched for their child or children. The wrenching sound of cries and whaling sobs merged as parents discovered their little ones. Several mothers overcome with grief and clouded judgment, cradled their badly injured child unaware the very act of holding them made the injuries worse. Others carried their children back home not realizing every available physician from nearby towns was at the school and that any medical attention at home was impossible. It was pandemonium, panic, a disaster of immeasurable proportions, and Andrew Kehoe was the cause.

Andrew Kehoe also caused the blast Martha and her group heard as they neared the front of the school. It was approximately thirty minutes after the main explosion that Kehoe drove his truck to the front of the school.

He saw one of the men he most detested, Emery Huyck, the school superintendent. Kehoe waved to him, calling him over. Unknown to Huyck, the truck was loaded with dynamite along with nails, farm tools, and other pieces of metal to be used as shrapnel. As Huyck approached, Kehoe pulled out his rifle and fired into the back igniting yet another huge fiery blast. The impact so powerful it decimated Kehoe's body hurling it down the road and across the street. It took time for people to find it.

Emory E. Huyck, School Superintendent

Remains of Andrew Kehoe's car

The explosion also instantly killed Superintendent Huyck. Kehoe's final act of madness ended in the death of two other men and a little boy who thought he had survived the blast. With that, one of America's greatest school tragedies had ended.

It was obvious the *Mad Murderer of Bath* planned this for some time. The amount of explosives was so vast it would have taken many trips to bring it in without being detected. By the time he was done, the entire basement of the school was wired. After a search of what remained of the school, more than five hundred pounds of dynamite had failed to go off. If those sticks of dynamite had ignited, it would have brought down the entire school. As terrible as this bombing was, it might have been much worse.

In the aftermath, investigations exposed the extent of Kehoe's madness. It was chilling. Kehoe had recently brought his wife back from one of her hospital stays. Before blowing up the school, Kehoe murdered his wife. The exact day and time of her death is unknown, but it definitely occurred before the school bombing. Then he unceremoniously dumped her body into a wooden hog cart and placed her behind the barn.

Destroyed cart where Nellie's remains were discovered.

With her in the cart was a box that contained their marriage certificate, money, silverware and other valuables. Before leaving, he went inside the barn and wired the legs of the horses together so they could not escape.

It was around 8:45 a.m. when Kehoe set off the firebombs on his property. The barn and house exploded into a raging inferno that sent huge billows of black smoke into the air. He wanted everything destroyed. Everything. Nothing of value would be left for anyone. Not Nellie's family, who still held ownership of the property, and not the people of Bath.

One of the neighbors saw Kehoe's farm burning. He and a friend were on their way to help with the fire and, instead, saw Kehoe behind the wheel of his truck leaving the farm. When he came up to them he stopped and called out, "Boys, you are my friends. You better get out of here. You better go down to the school." With that he drove off toward the school and his final plan of murder and suicide.

A coroner's report would later provide further details on the death of poor Nellie. Some believe he bludgeoned her on the head.

At the inquest, however, it was brought out that, upon examination, Nellie sustained only a slight crack to the skull without indentations. It was the type of crack that, according to the coroner's report, was consistent with head injuries sustained when subjected to extreme heat, such as the intensity of the fire that charred and partially cremated Nellie's body. It was also possible Kehoe had cut her throat. Because of the condition of her body, the exact cause of death could not be determined.

In his path of murder, Kehoe left one final message. It was carved out on a sign he'd wedged in between the wires of his fence. It read, "Criminals are made, not born."

Criminals are made, not born. Those words remained in our thoughts as we began our series of investigations. The profound tragedy of this event would make it one of the most difficult and troubling stories we've done. It compares only to the tragic Italian Hall Disaster in Calumet, Michigan, a story and investigation told in our second book.

The first investigation of Bath, Michigan, took place in the winter of 2008. We would meet up with Highland Ghost Hunters at Pleasant Hill Cemetery in Bath. This cemetery was one of the locations where many of the victims were interred. From there we would head down the road to Bath Memorial Park, site of the former Bath Consolidated School.

Because the investigations would be done late at night, Jenny Marcus and Lisa Mann, cofounders of Highland Ghost Hunters, got approval from the Bath Police Department to be in the cemetery. This is a very important requirement for any investigation done after hours.

That cold February evening was one we clearly remember. Temperatures headed downward but no one was thinking about that back then. All we saw were the rows of lonely gravestones. Too many tragic victims of Kehoe's madness.

Our flashlights scanned the headstones seeking out the infamous May 18, 1927, death date. It didn't take long. There were the names: Emma Nickols, Robert and Amelia (Emilie) Bromundt, LeVere Robert Harte, Robert Cushman, Katherine Foote, Floyd

Burnett, George and Lloyd Zimmerman, and many more. Our usual laughter and jokes were silent for this investigation.

Night vision cameras were positioned, and our small group spread out to conduct individual EVP sessions.

Sitting alone in the dark, I watched the full moon's faint light cast eerie shadows on the graveyard. The cold night's air crept into my jacket. Shivering, I pulled it closer and turned on the digital audio recorder. It would be a long evening. Indeed it was. We quietly moved from one lone grave site to another. As it would turn out, for this investigation, nothing happened. Not one unusual vision was seen nor an EVP captured.

A few hours later, we left and reassembled at the memorial site just off Webster Road. It is a surprisingly small, unassuming park. During the day, children play here and cars rush by, many never knowing or, worse, not caring about the site's significance.

The only reminders of its grim past are a few historical markers noting the event and the names of victims and, of course, the cupola. The still strong cupola was the masthead for the school sitting at the highest part of the roof. It now rested safely on the ground, the last remaining part of the original school. Its presence a constant reminder of May 18, 1927.

After the equipment was set up, our small group quietly wandered the grounds. It was upon these grounds the bodies of the deceased and injured were laid. It was here desperate, grief-stricken parents rushed to find their children.

Across the street was the current Bath Middle School. Moving to the front of the park to get a closer look, we stood on an old cement foundation. Initially everyone thought it might have been the remainder of a torn-down party store or gas station. The next day, however, Jenny discovered it was the foundation of a Quonset used by some students before the school was finally torn down.

After ninety minutes or so, we ended the hunt. What we quickly discovered is that it was very difficult to run a controlled investigation on the site. Although the town of Bath is still a relatively small community, Memorial Park fronts a very busy street. The loud rumbling of cars and trucks passing makes it extremely difficult to record audio. As it would turn out, like our cemetery investigation, nothing noteworthy was recorded; although, there was one photograph that quickly caught our attention.

It was a photo Bev had taken with her Canon Rebel SLR. Jenny was standing before the cupola. A series of bizarre lights fill the photo. Perhaps most eerie was a strong beam of light that originated from the top of the picture and angled straight in front of the cupola. Behind Jenny, toward the right side of the image, another interesting shape appeared. A light emerged from the ground and eerily took the shape of a human. It is a perfect example of what some would say is a ghostly apparition bathed in ethereal light.

A combination of reflected light and the camera's slow shutter
speed created this unusual photo of the Bath cupola.

Of the thousands of photos we've taken, this had to be one of the most bizarre. Could this picture have actually captured a true paranormal event or was there a logical explanation?

The short streaks of light in the distant background were easily identified. They were the street lamps that blurred as a result of slight hand movement and slow shutter speed. This is commonly found in night photography.

The straight beam of light streaming down from the top of the cupola and the ethereal figure behind Jenny, however, were not as easy to identify. We slowly went through the dozens of photos taken around the site that evening. The images lined up side by side on the computer's light board then merged to form a composite and, in doing that, the likely cause was discovered. It was not paranormal. Merely an uncanny series of coincidences that incorporated reflected light, hand movement blurs and lens angle.

What the composite picture revealed was a tall light pole extending over the cupola. The lamp wasn't seen in the mysterious photo but its light had bounced off the camera's lens creating the downward streak. The image behind Jenny that strangely resembled a spirit rising from the ground ended up being another reflection from someone's flashlight bouncing off of the stone beneath. It was not a ghost or paranormal in any way. It was, however, a great example of how night photography can be very tricky. If you don't understand your equipment and the surroundings and don't do careful review, something totally explainable can become paranormal.

This investigation, like many we conduct, ended up with no evidence. Nothing that would suggest spirits remained from that dreadful day. We hoped those who passed had moved on to a far more peaceful, joyful place than this earth.

Several years later, however, we were drawn back to this story. What drew us back? Call it unfinished business. During our earlier investigation, we were unable to locate the grave of Andrew Kehoe or his poor wife, Nellie. It was while researching another story that we came across death records of Andrew Kehoe and identified the location of his unmarked grave. We also learned why we couldn't find Nellie's grave. She was buried under her maiden name, Price, not Kehoe. Her family, most likely, did not want this good woman to be in any way connected to Andrew Kehoe, the *Mad Murderer of Bath.*

The research and investigation of this story would not be complete without time spent at both grave sites. We also decided to return to Pleasant Hill Cemetery and the Bath Memorial Park.

For this series of investigations, we tried a different approach and ran them during the day, not at night. We considered the possibility that activity may be more prevalent at the time of burial. Although funerals for the victims were scattered over several days, burials occurred in the afternoon. Our research revealed most of the formal burials at Pleasant Hill Cemetery occurred between the hours of 1:30 p.m. and 3:30 p.m.

Joining us on these investigations would be a friend and fellow investigator, Maria Aistrop. Maria has worked with us on other cases. Not only is she dedicated to paranormal research, but she is very effective at collecting and identifying suspect evidence.

It was around mid-January when we arrived at Pleasant Hill Cemetery. Temperatures were well below freezing. Ice-cold winds immediately assaulted us as we exited our car, quickly turning our cheeks and noses bright red. A fresh layer of snow crunched beneath our feet as we made our way onto the cemetery grounds.

A puff of frozen breath escaped Bev's lips as another gust of wind tore at her coat. She tightened the scarf around her neck and said, "It's going to be tough to record with this wind." Then moved passed me mumbling, "Why can't we pick warmer days to come here?"

I called out after her, "Well, we could investigate on the beach in Hawaii. That would be nice. Maybe with an umbrella drink." Bev threw back a sarcastic glance and headed to the back of the cemetery.

Maria, with equipment in hand, told me she was going to check out the other side of the cemetery, and the investigation began.

I wandered down one row and stopped before the headstone of Pauline Shirts. Pauline was a sixth grader at Bath school. She would have been eleven years old the day after the bombing. Pauline was a happy, friendly little girl. Her parents said she was always playing school at home and wanted to be a teacher when she grew up. Sadly, that would never be.

I set my audio recorder and Mel-Meter down and introduced myself to Pauline and the family members buried beside her. At first my questions did not mention the bombing but rather general questions you might ask any child. What kind of games did she like to play? Who was her favorite teacher? What was her favorite class? Who were her best friends?

The next series of questions gently led into the morning of the bombing. Followed by more probing questions. No response was received.

Pauline Shirts
5/19/16 to 5/18/27

After the first series, I remained silent recalling a story from one of the few survivors in Pauline's class. The lad had told authorities the last thing he recalled was hearing a loud noise and feeling a hard jolt. He didn't feel any pain until he woke up in the hospital and had no idea what had happened.

It is very likely those who died in the bombing did not know what had happened. As I contemplated the next series of questions, Bev approached. She pointed to a section at the back of the cemetery where we should go next. I nodded as we joined in a final session at Pauline's grave.

Starting again, I told Pauline we were authors and wanted to tell the story of her school's bombing. Bev said, "We don't want anyone to forget you."

I asked if she remembered what occurred at her school that day. Then followed with, "Andrew Kehoe is the man who blew up the school. Did you know that?"

Bev and I went on to tell her about Kehoe and his story of madness and revenge. What we didn't know at the time is that, after we asked if she knew who Andrew Kehoe was, a soft, urgent EVP was captured, "No."

We hoped she heard our explanation. Knowing who Kehoe was and what happened may have helped her understand and, in that, provide her with some peace.

Our next section was at the back of the cemetery, the section Bev had pointed out earlier. It was the grave of Katherine Foote. Katherine was ten years old when she perished. Like her classmate, Pauline Shirts, she was determined to be a teacher when she grew up. Nothing would have stopped her from achieving that goal if not for the bomb on May 18, 1927.

We stood at Katherine's grave site and looked down at her well-worn headstone. Many of the Bath victim grave markers have been restored or replaced. Katherine's, however, had not. Her name and date of birth and death were worn and marked with the passing of time.

Katherine Foote:
5/29/17 to 5/18/27

We spent some time at Katherine's grave without evidence or even a slight sign of response. Until, that is, we were about to leave. Bev and Maria were headed to the next victim's burial site. I held back for a moment.

I offered one last question. "Katherine Foote, talk to me. What happened?" Without response, I walked away. As I turned to leave, my audio recorder captured one revealing EVP.

"No one told me."

Maria was checking out a few other locations in the cemetery, then joined the two of us as we headed toward Emma Nickol's grave. Emma was thirteen years old and just a few days away from completing sixth grade. Her two younger sisters, Ruth and Otelia, were also at the school that day. Although her younger sisters were injured, they both survived the blast. Emma did not.

(L to R) Bev and Maria asking questions of two students

Bev, Maria, and I took turns asking questions and waiting for responses that were unheard. Similar to Katherine Foote, a most important piece of audio evidence was captured near the time our session at her grave was over.

I asked, "Emma Nickols, are you at peace now?"

The response was strong. "No!" The word that followed, "Momma!" Whether the energy was residual or intelligent is not known. The response, however, was a powerful reminder of an emotional imprint left by a frightened little girl.

(L to R) Ruth Nickols, injured; Otelia Nickols, injured;
Emma Nickols: 7/16/14 to 5/18/27

Before heading to our next stop, Bath Memorial Park, we stopped for one last session. It was the grave site of eleven-year-old Emilie (Amelia) and thirteen-year-old Robert Bromundt. Both brother and sister perished in the blast.

Amelia loved school and was a quick learner. Her brother, on the other hand, was not. He thought school was tedious and would have much-preferred working on the farm with his father or playing baseball with his friends. That morning, both were in their classrooms on the north wing, the section of the school that collapsed after the explosion.

Amelia Bromundt: 1/22/16 to 5/18/27
Robert Bromundt: 8/2/14 to 5/18/27

Class was in full session when the building shook from the loud explosion that rocked the very foundations of the school, throwing the children upward from their seats. According to one report, the roof seemed to literally open up with the full sky exposed; then, from seemingly nowhere, the roof came crashing back down. The weight from the debris caused the second floor to collapse to the first where the sixth grade classes were. Amelia and Robert Bromundt were killed along with most of their classmates.

One of the few survivors, Ada Dolton would later say it didn't hurt at all. Rather, it felt as though she were floating. She looked up and saw all the other children along with their desks moving upward, as if they were flying through space.

Amelia and Robert's older brother, Rudy Bromundt, was spared a similar fate. He was a high school student at Bath. Fortunately, he was not in the deadly north wing. In spite of that, however, his classroom shuddered wildly, windows exploded, and ceiling plaster fell. The entire building seemed to rock.

In panic, without thinking, Rudy jumped from an upper floor window landing on the ground below. He began to run. He didn't know where he was running—just away from the school. In fact, the young man ran past his home and continued running. His father saw him run past the house, so he got in his car and chased after him. Only later did they discover both of Rudy's legs had been broken in his fall. Running had permanently damaged his legs. He walked with a limp the rest of his life.

The funerals of the Bromundt children occurred on Saturday at 1:30 p.m. Their remains were interred some time afterwards. I glanced at my watch. It was 2:30. The session began.

We introduced ourselves, told the children not to be afraid, and encouraged them to speak with us. Maria explained that the devices in our hands would allow us to communicate with them.

Maria also placed a toy on the ground she had brought with her. It was a type of Spirograph with a free-floating drawing wheel. When the wheel was pushed, it would draw pictures or spell words. Maria carefully demonstrated how to use the toy encouraging the spirits to have fun with it. We backed away as our session began.

I asked Robert if they called him by that name or a nickname, like Bob or Robbie. Then asked a similar question to Amelia.

"Amelia? Did they call you Amy or Amelia?" Pausing briefly, I continue. "Is your last name Bromundt?"

Maria quickly cut in, "I swear I just heard something that way." She waved her hand in front of her and to the left.

Maria was right. Listening to audio playback we captured a child's voice. It said, "Mellie." Could that have been Amelia's nickname? A week or so later we discovered a genealogy page where family descendants confirmed Amelia's nickname was indeed Mellie.

One other audio clip was recorded during our session at the Bromundt site. I asked, "What was your favorite class in school?" Maria followed, "Did you have a favorite teacher? One that was real nice?" What we captured was a soft, sweet voice, clearly a little girl's whisper that said, "Mrs. Harte."

Blanche Harte, Teacher:
5/18/27

There was indeed a Bath school teacher named Harte. Mrs. Blanche Harte was Amelia Bromundt's teacher and happened to be leading the classroom at the time of the bombing. Mrs. Harte died along with most of her students that day. This EVP remains as an undeniable confirmation that Amelia had communicated with us this day.

We must admit to heartache as we left Pleasant Hill Cemetery. It is incredibly difficult to think that even one young spirit remains fearful or lost. Although we explained to each what happened that fatal day and encouraged them to move into the light where loved ones waited, who knows if they heard or if it helped. Certainly others, over the decades, have done the same. For whatever reason they have not all moved on. Perhaps one day they will. We pray one day they will.

The next stop on our investigation was Memorial Park, site of the former Bath Consolidated School. There was a certain reverence as we slowly walked the grounds and stood by the old school's cupola.

We stayed here only a short time, just a little over thirty minutes. Unfortunately, traffic noise continued to be a real problem. Time was running late. With the three of us chilled to the bone, temperatures rapidly dropping, and even stronger winds coming in from the west, it was time to wrap. We headed to the warmth of the car and made our way home. Later review would reveal no evidence captured.

Another trip was scheduled for March 8th. On that day we would culminate the investigation at the grave sites of Andrew Kehoe and his wife, Nellie.

The sky was perfectly blue as we made our way to Lansing and the Mount Hope Cemetery where the remains of Ellen (Nellie) Price Kehoe rests. She is buried in her family's plot under her maiden name, Ellen A. Price. Her family purposefully omitted Nellie's married name, not wanting her to be connected in any way to her demented husband.

Although the Price family burial site is found deep within the cemetery, the tall, impressive, mausoleum with the word "Price" embedded above the door makes it stand out from other family plots. Most of the Price family surrounded the Mausoleum; Nellie's grave was one of them.

Nellie Price Kehoe

Bev, Maria, and I gathered around and respectfully stood in silence for a few moments. Ellen Agnes Price, known to friends and family as Nellie, remained single until 1912 when, at the age of 34, she married Andrew Kehoe. Waiting so long to marry was quite unusual back in those days, especially for a woman coming from a prominent family.

At 34, Nellie would have been considered a *spinster or old maid*. A term dreaded by most young girls in those days. It spoke of a woman well beyond the conventional age of marriage, unwanted by men, and likely to remain single the rest of their life. To be unmarried at the age of 34 was considered a sad fate.

Was it Nellie's choice to remain single? Was she a woman who enjoyed her independence? Was she a woman ahead of her time that didn't need or want a man to take care of her? Might it have been something else that kept her single?

Years before, she and Andrew had been courting. After he headed west, their courtship ended. Was it possible she had pined for him through those years? Had she thought of Andrew Kehoe as her one true love?

Shortly after the untimely death of his stepmother, Andrew resumed his courtship of Nellie. Within months they were wed. Did love bring them together or was it merely a marriage of convenience? Convenient for Kehoe because Nellie's family had money; convenient for Nellie because it was expected a woman should marry.

It was frustrating. Our research turned up nothing that would help us better understand the relationship between Nellie Price and Andrew Kehoe. Nellie had been involved in social and church groups. That involvement began to cease several years into the marriage. It was said Andrew Kehoe was the reason for it.

What kind of life did she lead? God knows she had serious health problems. Adding to that was this emotionally volatile man who could be nice one moment and explode in anger the next, especially if she disagreed with him. It must have placed a terrible burden on her already troubled life.

Our investigation at the Price burial grounds began. We introduced ourselves explaining our intentions of getting Nellie's side of the story.

"Nellie," I asked. "What we want to do is talk with you to find out what you remember on that day so when we write our story we can tell it accurately."

"What are your last memories?" Bev, Maria, and I waited in silence. Only the distant sound of passing birds was heard.

I continued, "Had he talked to you about his feeling regarding the taxes going up? What do you remember on that May day in 1927?"

With no response, Bev took her turn, pausing between each question. "When did you find out he was going to do it? Did you know the day before, minutes before or, maybe never?"

Maria was next. "Were you afraid of Andrew? Did he scare you? Was he afraid to have children or could you not have them?"

Our questions continued without evidence that Nellie's spirit was with us that afternoon. We hoped her soul had moved on and she was at peace. She deserved that.

It was time to move on to our last destination, Mount Rest Cemetery in St. Johns, and the burial site of Andrew Kehoe. The exact location of Kehoe's grave remains unknown to this day. Even cemetery offices were unable to provide details.

Of course, there are some who claim to know exactly where he's buried, but that is unlikely. After the bombing, a family member authorized Kehoe's remains be transported to Mount Rest Cemetery and buried in the pauper's section. There are two men who know with certainty where he lies. That would be the grave digger and Andrew Kehoe. Both are now long dead.

Melting, crusted snow crunched beneath our feet as we made our way to the pauper's section. Most of the graves markers in this area are small. The simple markers had names inscribed and, at least, year of death. That's the nature of a paupers' grave. Those buried were poor, indigent, or simply unknown. The county handled most, if not all, of the cost of burial. Therefore, grave sites were kept cheap with simple headstones and wooden box coffins.

There is an area in the far corner without a grave marker. That is where we believe Andrew Kehoe's body remains. We set up for our investigation in that area.

(L to R) Maria and Kat asking Andrew why he
would do such a horrible thing.

I began by calling out his name. "Andrew Kehoe. Andrew Kehoe. Are you here, Mr. Kehoe? Andrew Kehoe, can you come forward?"

"You are the man who set the bombs in May 1927. Are you here? Come forward. We want to talk to you in order to understand what you did."

Maria encouraged him, "Andrew can you come forward and talk to us? Andrew can you tell us why you blew up the school in Bath, Michigan? Can you tell us why you had to take the lives of so many innocent children?"

Questions continued to be asked regarding his motives, but all remained quiet. Maria changed her questions asking about his wife, Nellie.

"Why did you kill your wife, Andrew? What did she do to you other than being sick? When you got married, didn't you know it was for better or worse, in sickness and in health? She was sick, and you couldn't handle it so you decided to go ahead and kill her. Smack her in the head; throw her in a wheelbarrow like she was nothing."

But even Maria's aggressive questions didn't stir a response. Kehoe remained elusive.

The questions turned to Andrew not having children. Maria wondered if he missed not having them around. She wondered if he missed not having their small arms around his neck calling in daddy.

Without a response, Bev decided to take a different tact. It was very possible Andrew Kehoe did not like children. "You hated children, didn't you, Andrew? You didn't want someone to call you daddy."

Maria added, "Did you have a bad childhood? Is that why, maybe? You were afraid you'd be like your own father. Was he mean to you?"

Suddenly Bev's K2 meter started hitting, its lights flashing rapidly several times.

"Andrew, did I hit a nail on a head when I said that?" Maria asked. We hoped for another EMF response but it didn't come.

I followed Bev's line of thought, "Maybe Bev was right. You didn't want kids. You don't like kids. Children are self-centered..."

Bev called out, "K2 full red."

I continued. "Children are self-centered, useless, unimportant, spoiled little brats. You didn't like them, did you Andrew?" The K2 lights continued to flicker then went dark.

I moved closer to Bev, "Andrew Kehoe are you here?" There was a sudden stillness in the air. Even the chirping birds quieted. That's when Maria's recorder captured our first EVP. It said, "Yes."

"Andrew," Maria continued. "If you're here can you say yes when I count to three, loud enough for us to hear. One … two … three …"

Our eyes scanned the area looking for anything out of the ordinary. "Andrew?" Maria asked.

Another EVP followed, this one quieter. Later, when we listened to it during review, we needed to press headphones tightly to our ears. We heard the first word, "Andrew" but the second was more elusive. Was it "killer" or "killed her?" Could it even be "Kehoe?" This audio clip is included in our Secret Room. Listen to it and decide for yourself.

For the next thirty minutes our questions focused on Kehoe's relationship with women, his wife, feelings about taxes and the Bath school. Nothing. It seemed whatever energy may have been building was gone.

I decided to move the questions away from Bath. Perhaps something completely different would get a response.

"What does it look like where you are right now? Do you see earth or is it different?"

It was then Maria's recorder captured a very compelling EVP. One of the many she sent to us after her audio review. She told us there were three words, "I see everything." For Bev and I, the first portion of the EVP was difficult to understand. However, the last word "…everything" was clear. Very interesting.

Quantum theory suggests there exists one or more dimensions beyond the three dimensions our eyes can see. A few leading-edge physicists are attempting to determine the viability of this theory. It is sometimes referred to as String Theory.

If theorists are correct, other dimensions may hold the answer to life after physical body death. Some believe our life energies transition to another dimension in which time has no relevance. Spirits or beings can see from the beginning of time and look ahead to a limitless future. It is a completely different state of existence and something that escapes those of us on earth, locked within our three-dimension world. Quantum theorists suggest those within these other dimensions can see everything. Does this EVP suggest theorists are correct?

Our questions ended for a time as the three of us quietly observed the surrounding area. Eventually, another session started.

The only time EMF levels spiked was when we brought up the subject of Kehoe's hard life and possible dislike of children and parents. Our new line of questions returned to that subject.

In a firm, slightly agitated voice I began, "Those kids were spoiled. That's why you had to do it. Kids are spoiled! Parents spoil them. Parents voted in the taxes to spoil their kids even more!" Then, in a matter-of-fact way finished, "You had to do what you had to do."

I glanced at Bev and Maria to see if EMF levels had been affected. They shook their heads. I continued, more resolute.

"But you were wrong to do that. You know that. You were sick, Andrew. I hope God has forgiven you."

Bev added, "God is the only one who will forgive you. The people in Bath hate you."

I agreed, "That's right, Andrew. The only other ones who could forgive you … they're dead too. The only one who can forgive you now is God. Did God forgive you, Andrew?"

Seconds passed. Bev pushed for an answer. "Mr. Kehoe, respond to us please." We waited, watched. Silence followed.

Mid-afternoon soon passed to late afternoon. The sun was cooling as it made its downward descent and a cold wind swept through. We would need to leave soon.

A few, final questions were asked. What we wouldn't know at the time is that those last questions would result in giving us our most significant evidence. Possibly answering questions many have wondered for decades.

"Mr. Kehoe, are you happy where you are now? Are you afraid or sad? Are you hurting?"

The EVP was captured by Maria. She would send it to us for further review. Placing the headphones on, I heard the hiss of white noise and buried within it the first part of the EVP. Pressing the headphones tight against my ears, I repeated the audio clip several times. It sounded very much like, "Yes, I am hurting and …" The voice paused for a moment, possibly to build strength. The next word was loud, powerful, and aggressive. "ANGRY!"

"Wow!" I said, quickly pulling away the headphones and handing them to Bev. Her eyes widened as she glanced at me and nodded. "He is definitely angry."

There was one last question that needed to be asked before we left on that late winter afternoon. "Andrew Kehoe, do you regret killing those children?"

Maria's recorder picked up the final response. The word was raspy but firm. "Yes!" He said.

This EVP ends our story. There are still too many unanswered questions. There always are in tragedies like this. What causes a mind to twist into something so perversely dark and deadly? Even Andrew Kehoe may not know but, then again, maybe he does.

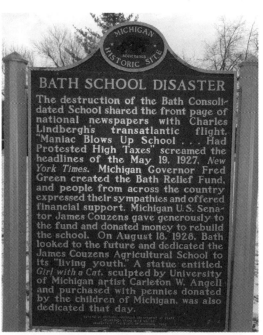

BATH SCHOOL DISASTER

The destruction of the Bath Consolidated School shared the front page of national newspapers with Charles Lindbergh's transatlantic flight. "Maniac Blows Up School . . . Had Protested High Taxes" screamed the headlines of the May 19, 1927, *New York Times*. Michigan Governor Fred Green created the Bath Relief Fund, and people from across the country expressed their sympathies and offered financial support. Michigan U.S. Senator James Couzens gave generously to the fund and donated money to rebuild the school. On August 18, 1928, Bath looked to the future and dedicated the James Couzens Agricultural School to its "living youth." A statue entitled, *Girl with a Cat*, sculpted by University of Michigan artist Carleton W. Angell and purchased with pennies donated by the children of Michigan, was also dedicated that day.

In Memory Of Those Lost
To you go our thoughts and prayers.

Arnold V. Bauerle
Henry and Herman Bergan
Emilie (Mellie) M. and Robert Bromundt
Floyd E. Burnett
Russell J. Chapman
G. Cleo Clayton
F. Robert Cochran
Ralph A. Cushman
Earl E. Ewing
Katherine O. Foote
Marjorie and Richard Fritz
Carlyle W. Geisenhaver
Beatrice P. Gibbs
George P. Hall, Jr.
Willa M. and Iola I. Hart
Percy E. and Vivian O. Hart
Blanche E. Harte
Galen L., LaVere R., Stanley H. Harte
Francis O. Hoeppner
Cecial L. Hunter
Emory E. Huyck
Doris E. Johns
Nellie Kehoe
Thelma I. MacDonald
Clarence W. and Nelson McFarren
J. Emerson Medcoff
Emma A. Nickols
Richard D. Richardson
Elsie M. Robb
Pauline M. Shirts
Glenn O. Smith
Hazel I. Weatherby
Elizabeth J. and Lucille J. Witchell
Harold L. Woodman
George O. and Lloyd Zimmerman

Story Two:
Lady of the Lake

Townline Lake
Big Rapids, MI

Password: nor918

A SIMPLE GHOST STORY, SHARED BETWEEN friends over dinner, led us to one of our most remarkable cases. An urban legend became more than a ghost story; it became a confirmation of abiding love and a testament to the bravery of soldiers at war.

It began on a Sunday afternoon. Bev and I were headed back from a weekend investigation in northern Michigan. Tired and hungry, we decided to stop for something to eat before continuing home. It was purely a matter of time and chance that we found ourselves in Big Rapids. The Applebee's Restaurant seemed as good a place as any.

The hostess took us to a booth near a table with four ladies of ranging ages. They were laughing and generally having a great time. We briefly smiled at the friendly group then turned our attention to the menu. Some time later, after placing our order, Bev and I sat in silence. Really, after a long drive and an even longer weekend, there was nothing more to talk about. As the saying goes, silence is golden.

That is when we became aware of the conversation at the nearby table. With just a touch of sarcastic humor, we heard one of the women ask another, "I heard you saw that ghost again."

"Ghost?" Bev and I glanced at each other. Like a moth to a flame, we were instantly and secretly drawn into their conversation.

An older woman responded, with a slight wave of her hand. "Go ahead and laugh. I'm old enough not to care anymore. But I saw her. She was there and she was real. I saw her before, years ago. It was the same girl. She looked just like I remember. I think she's been wandering out there for years and years and probably will forever."

One of the women, obviously as uninformed as Bev and I, asked "What are you talking about? What ghost? What girl by the lake?"

The older woman just shrugged as she took a sip from her glass. Another woman at the table answered for her.

"The Lady of the Lake. There's supposed to be this ghost girl wandering around Townline Lake, waiting for her soldier boyfriend to come home."

The younger woman nodded, a smile edging its way to the corners of her mouth. "Oh. Got it."

The older woman sensed the oozing skepticism and firmly set her glass down. "Well, just because you girls haven't seen her doesn't mean she's not there."

Bev raised an eyebrow and I nodded in silent agreement. She leaned toward the table and said hello. With very little prodding, the older woman happily introduced us to the legend of the Lady of the Lake. That is when this journey began.

As the story goes, there was a young girl by the name of Florence who, at the tender age of sixteen, met and fell in love with a young man. They grew deeply in love and vowed they would marry as soon as the girl was old enough.

Then came 1917 and World War I. America joined the fight in the *War to End All Wars*. The young man was compelled to serve his country and joined in the fight for freedom.

He enlisted in the military against the girl's wishes. On a hot summer day, shortly before he left for training, they met at their favorite meeting place, Townline Lake, and vowed their eternal love.

The girl begged him, one last time, not to go. Consoling her, he told her not to worry. He would return; they would marry and spend the rest of their lives together. Forever. Unfortunately, as fate would have it, the young man died in battle.

The girl was so distraught and broken hearted over her love's death that one day she wandered to their meeting place at Townline Lake, walked into the water, and ended her life. It is said her spirit still wanders the area around Townline and is sometimes seen standing near the water's edge waiting for her man to return.

When the woman finished the story, the entire table was silent for several long seconds. It really was quite a good story, ghost or no ghost. I asked her where she'd heard the tale. She said from her mother who had heard it from her mother.

Was any of it true? She didn't know. All she knew is that she'd seen what appeared to be the apparition of a young woman twice in her life. The vision appeared out of nowhere and vanished as quickly.

We thanked them and returned to our table where dinner had just arrived. Over the meal, Bev and I discussed the story. It was, of course, just another urban legend. Yet, often within the fiction of legend there is an element of truth. Had the woman really seen an apparition of this heartbroken young woman?

In spite of the fact that we were tired, we decided to delay the journey home for a short time and check it out. Townline Lake wasn't far.

Though Townline is a smaller lake, it does have reported depths up to fifty-two feet. Located in Colfax Township, next to Big Rapids, it is a popular fishing lake with an abundance of bass, bluegill, northern pike, and crappie.

Because of its size, the lake goes largely unnoticed by many travelers coming to Mecosta County. We drove down a few miles of scenic country roads, passing farms and woodlands. It is still very much a rural area.

It wasn't long before we found the public access sign to Townline and pulled in. Stepping out onto the dock we scanned the scene before us. It was beautiful. Late afternoon sun was beginning to slip low in the sky. Its warm light sprinkled across the water's gentle ripples. The area across from us was densely wooded with only a scattering of homes seen on the shoreline.

We noted two homes on either side of us just beyond the covering of trees. From what we could see, the homes were shut tight and all was silent, very still. The dozen or so homes around the lake also seemed empty with not a single boat on the water. The two of us were completely alone.

It was a bit breezy that afternoon. Wind rustling through the trees merging with the sounds of chirping birds and nature. Capturing good EVPs would be a challenge with all of this ambient sound.

We made our way slowly through brush and trees hoping their covering would cut the wind contamination. Our EVP session began.

I would like to say we had a feeling or sensed something unusual. We did not. It was actually a very peaceful, calming area.

Our questions were vague and, because we were more than a little tired, uncreative. What is your name? Are you waiting for your boyfriend to return? What is your boyfriend's name? Was your boyfriend killed in the war?

Throughout it all, EMF levels remained flat. Nothing was heard but wind rustling the leaves and the muffled cries of a child. A child?

Turning to Bev I asked, "Is that a baby I hear crying or ... do you hear a baby?"

Listening for a few moments, she responded. "I might."

"What is that? A woman? A baby?"

We checked the homes on either side. Windows and doors were closed and no cars in the parking area. The quiet cries were clearly not coming from either house.

Bev suggested we go out to the dock and scanned the area. Although the homes around the lake appeared vacant, there was a brisk wind, and sounds can carry.

The actual source of the sound remained elusive as the muffled cries continued. The more we listened, the more it seemed less a child and more a woman.

I stepped onto the dock with a K2 in one hand and an audio recorder in the other. "Is there someone with us here on the lake? Did your boyfriend die in World War I? Is that true?"

With no apparent response, I turned my attention to the lake and the heavily wooded section of land directly across.

If any of the legend was true, where had the young woman been when she ended her life? It may have been the area now designated as public access or, frankly, anywhere around the lake. If our research turned up the suicide of young Florence, perhaps we'd get a better idea on the location.

Our EVP session continued, remaining uneventful until I heard Bev's startled whisper. "Oh my God."

I turned to see her surprised expression as she pointed to a small cluster of trees and shrubs to the right. "My God, I think I just saw something there."

Since Bev had never before claimed to actually see a suspect vision, this was really unusual. I immediately took note. The surprised look in her eyes told me she was being completely truthful.

I asked her what she'd seen. She wasn't certain. It was just out of the corner of her eyes. A fleeting image that was there and gone.

We headed to the area where the movement had been seen. Nothing now. I glanced down at my recorder to make sure it was still running and was surprised to see the battery had been completely drained. A fresh battery had been inserted just before we left the car not 15 or 20 minutes before. It was cool outside but not so cold as to drain a battery that quickly. Curious.

We searched through the small cluster of trees and scrubs. Nothing. Again, we looked at the homes on either side. They were dark. Windows and doors shut.

The wind grew even stronger, making the likelihood of good EVP recordings unlikely. Bev and I decided to head back to the warmth of the car and home.

In the next few days, we forgot our brief session at Townline Lake. We focused, instead, on our previous weekend's investigation. After hours of audio and video review, nothing significant turned up for that weekend's investigation. There were no suspect EVP's or compelling video, just a lot of white noise and strained eyes. This was typical of many investigations.

There was one last audio segment left. I settled the headphones against my aching ears again and cued it up. The sound of wind immediately filled my ears. That's when I realized the audio was from our brief time at Townline Lake.

Wind. Lots of wind. I silently shook my head in disappointment. Just as we'd feared, contaminated audio. It seemed our time at the lake would be a bust. I listened anyway. You have to. There could be breaks in the wind where an EVP may be captured.

Indeed, there were occasional breaks in the wind. I could hear Bev and I talking and the sound of my chuckle as I teased her for use of uncreative EVP questions. I smiled to myself, hearing her throw back a sarcastic remark. Typical.

I remembered it was not long after her sarcastic retort that the strange crying was heard. I became more alert, pressing earphones close. Nothing. If there was crying, it was too soft and the wind too strong.

Frustrated. Then, moments later, through the rush of the wind a voice was heard. It was definitely not Bev or I. What did it say?

I continued to listen. More words. So quiet. Was it just anomalous sounds my mind was converting into words, or had we captured an actual EVP?

Isolating the suspect audio clips, I called Bev to come and listen. She pressed the headphones to her ears as the audio played over and over. Bev looked at me, a question in her eyes, but I could tell she heard the words too. We had to go back.

"Help her… help me." The quiet words whispered. It was not a desperate call for help but rather a quiet request.

Because of schedules, the return trip would be delayed for a while. In the meantime, research to find the Lady of the Lake began. Was there a Florence who had loved a World War I soldier? Did this soldier die in the war, and did she kill herself at Townline Lake. It was like searching for a strand of hair in the ocean. Where to begin?

After long weeks of frustrating research, nothing was discovered. Although there had been a few reported drownings around Townline Lake in the World War I time frame, none were considered suicides and none of the victims were named Florence.

In spite of any evidence to validate the existence of Florence or her soldier boy lover, the EVP that said, "Help me … help her," drew us back to the lake again. We may not have found Florence or the Lady of the Lake, but it's possible we stumbled upon something else. Someone was seeking help.

It was December when we returned. The early afternoon air was chilled and the area again silent.

Since the surrounding woodlands appeared to be blocked off, likely private land, we decided to return to the public access area. Bev and I pulled our coats up close around us as we began another EVP session. We stayed for well over an hour returning to the car briefly to warm our numb fingers before heading back again. The wind was another challenge this day. We attempted to use our bodies to block gusts that swept in from the lake.

Audio review began the next day. It was in the last few minutes of audio that something very curious was captured. We had gone out to the edge of the lake and, for the last time asked, "If there is a lady with us, tell us your name." What followed was a single word, "Allie." A second or two later, the word again, "Allie."

Allie? Could our Lady of the Lake actually be named Allie and not Florence as the legend goes? We headed back to historical records. Although we found no one named Florence who died in the area around World War I, we did discover a connection to the drowning death of someone named Allie at Townline Lake.

It seemed an impossible task. Countless hours were spent. We were about to give up and then, as if by some divine intervention, we came across a very small article in the *Jackson Citizen Patriot* dated August 12, 1918. It was titled, "Big Rapids Girl Drowns in Townline Lake."

The article was very brief:

> *"Miss Alvena Holen, 17 years old, daughter of Mrs. A. Holen, was drowned in Town Line lake two miles northeast of here Sunday afternoon. The body was recovered."*

The next day we found her death certificate. The actual name on record was "Almina Holen," not Alvena. Newspapers are frequently wrong.

Recorded date of death was August 11, 1918, and the cause "accidental drowning." Allie could certainly be a nickname for Almina. It was not much to go on, but there was a name and a drowning death on Townline Lake. We took what we had and ran with it.

What followed were more weeks of research. Slowly, very slowly, the layers peeled away and pieces of the puzzled formed a clear picture. It became our most incredible true-life journey. So begins this most remarkable story.

To tell this story properly, we need to go back more than a decade before World War I. To an innocent and relatively carefree time in Big Rapids and its neighboring town of Colfax

It's the early 1900s. Back then, Big Rapids was quickly growing. Construction of hydro-electric dams brought electricity to the community strengthening logging, furniture building, and other wood product manufacturing businesses.

Big Rapids at turn of the century

Education was also booming. The move toward higher education was led by Woodbridge Ferris who, in 1884, established Ferris State Industrial School (now Ferris State University). Mr. Ferris would, in 1912, become Governor of Michigan.

This was also a time when business owners began giving employees more free time. From this extra free time came vacations and tourism. Big Rapids and Colfax, with several beautiful lakes, became a popular spot for vacationers. The big draw was Clear Lake, one of the larger lakes in the community.

In spite of their rapidly growing sizes, the communities of Big Rapids and Colfax still maintained their small-town charm. Everyone knew everyone. That's just the way it was back then, and town folk wanted to keep it that way.

In summer months, residents of Big Rapids and Colfax avoided Clear Lake and its throng of tourists. Instead, the *townies* headed to the smaller, relatively unnoticed Townline Lake.

Little Allie and her family were *townies*. Her father, August, and mother, Chistena, operated a small farm next to Townline Lake. The farm and lake were just about all little Allie ever knew.

August and Chistena were blessed with eight children. Allie was the second youngest. In their early years, older siblings handled much of the heavy chores on the farm. Her oldest brother, Alvin, almost nine years Allie's senior, took the lead helping his father and mother operate the farm.

In many ways Alvin was like a second father to his brothers and sisters. With a great sense of humor and calm demeanor, he always seemed to know what to do. Allie loved him and, like the other children, came to depend on him as much as she did her parents.

Of course, during the hot summer months Allie's family would head to Townline Lake. For the little girl, spending the day at the lake was one of the greatest pleasures she knew.

Then, of course, there was Norman. Norman was not related by blood. He was Alvin's best friend and seemed like part of the family.

Allie loved when Norman came by. She enjoyed watching Alvin and Norman rough-house in the water. The two of them made her laugh.

There was another reason Allie liked having Norman around. It was a secret she shared with no one. Allie thought Norman was just about the nicest looking boy she'd ever seen. He was athletic, tall with blue eyes and light brown hair. Even to her little girl's eyes, Norman was nearly as perfect as a boy could be.

It was late summer, 1913. Allie was twelve years old. The shorter days and cooler nights heralded the end of summer and time along the shores of Townline Lake.

Crops needed harvesting, and the family was spending longer hours in the fields. That September Allie was a little sad knowing her brother Alvin would soon be going off to college. She would miss him very much. What she didn't know was that something was about to happen that would delay Alvin's leaving and throw the family in turmoil.

Their father became ill. At first it was thought he was suffering from indigestion or the stomach flu. It was when his weakness grew, stomach cramps worsened, and his fever soared that the family became alarmed. The doctor came. The prognosis was not good: typhoid fever.

The next six weeks were difficult for everyone as August struggled with this horrible illness. Finally, in early November, complications from the disease ended his life.

The entire family was grief-stricken. His death was an immeasurable loss to his wife and children. Adding to their emotional state, he was in charge of the farm. Now what would they do? Chistena was a strong woman, but with eight children would she be able to manage the farm alone and still take care of the family?

Alvin stepped in. As the oldest son, it was his responsibility

His mother protested. She told him he had to go to college. That is what August had wanted and that is what she wanted. Certainly farming was not Alvin's career choice. After college he'd hope to find a career in business or education, but family came first.

For the first year after his father's passing, he helped his mother manage the farm. The second year Chistena's brother took over leaving Alvin free to attend college. He enrolled in State Normal School, now known as Eastern State University.

Allie was forlorn the day Alvin left. Without her father or Alvin, the house seemed darker. Empty.

All was not lost to Allie. There was Norman. Beautiful Norman. Instead of going away to college like his friend Alvin, Norman decided to attend nearby Ferris College while working at his father's wood veneer business. He made it a point to stop by the farm from time to time to say hello.

Alvin Holen

Meanwhile, at State Normal, Alvin was finding a whole new way of life. It was the first time he was away from home and everything was different. He enjoyed his independence and the challenge of education.

It was while in school he met a remarkable young woman. Her name was Theda. She was a compassionate, intelligent beauty, strong with her own mind and great wit. Her confidence and straight-forward personality stood out among the other young women, especially at a time when ladies were not expected to have strong opinions. Theda was happy to debate anyone on almost any topic—and she usually won.

Theda was indeed different, and Alvin was immediately attracted. It wasn't long before they were completely in love.

The summer of 1915 was a happy one for Allie and her family. Chistena had taken to running the farm with her brother, and they were getting by fairly well. Alvin had completed his education and accepted an excellent position as principal at a school in southern Michigan, close to where Theda lived. The job was a distance from the family, but it was a wonderful position. Alvin promised he'd visit often, and he did—especially in the summer months. The family once again shared laughter and good times at Townline Lake.

At the age of fourteen, Allie was very happy. Her brother had Theda and Allie had Norman. Well, she *almost* had Norman. Although she had matured since her father's passing, she was still too young. But, in her mind, they were destined to be together. Life seemed bright with wonderful opportunities and endless happiness.

That summer no one thought much about the war in Europe. The fighting did not touch the quiet shores of Townline Lake. It was, after all, Europe's war not America's.

Then came 1916. Things began to change. Fighting overseas escalated. Rumblings began in Congress about America joining the fight. President Woodrow Wilson was also contemplating the likelihood of the United States' involvement in the war.

Though dark storm clouds may have been approaching America, the waters of Townline were as blue and calm as ever and the fishing still great. The summer of 1916 would be the last summer of innocence for the townies of Mecosta County and, perhaps, America.

In April 1917, a British cruise and transport ship called the *Lusitania* left the docks of New York headed to Britain. German U-boats attacked and sunk the ship killing 1195 people. Of those, 128 were Americans.

The United States could no longer remain neutral. President Wilson emphasized the need for America to make the world safe for democracy and asked Congress to declare war. It would be The Great War, *The War to End All Wars*. Patriotism was at an all-time high. Young men lined up at recruiting offices ready to fight for democracy and their country.

When Alvin and Norman heard the news, they knew they had to serve. There was no question. As patriots and Americans, they had to fight for this great cause.

Theda, an advocate against war, was upset when Alvin told her his decision. As he spoke, his passion and commitment was obvious and her heart sank. Theda had won many debates in school. This was one debate she would lose. All the love they shared would not change that. So, Theda did what love made her do. She accepted his decision and prayed for his safety.

When Alvin announced his decision to the family, his mother, Chistena, was stoic. We can only imagine Allie's reaction. Alvin remained her solid rock in the family. Making things even worse, Norman would also be going. Both men would put their lives in jeopardy to fight and perhaps die in a war Allie did not really understand. So on June 5, 1917, Alvin and Norman enlisted. It was their last summer of innocence along the shores of Townline Lake.

Both young men were accepted into the officer's training program at Fort Sheridan. The day of his departure, Alvin presented Theda with a single rose. A single rose was the symbol of their love, simple and beautiful.

Before Norman's departure, the dream Allie had secretly carried since childhood came true. He professed his affection. For Allie it was a moment of profound joy and sadness. After the war, Norman promised he'd return. She prayed it would be true.

And so it was Alvin and Norman left for officer's training. For the family back home, the waiting began. Weeks seemed like years. Finally, word came from Alvin. He gave the good news first. He and Norman had completed officers training. More good news; they would be home for Christmas. The good news ended there. He next shared the fact that shortly after the first of the year, they would be sailing for France.

The Christmas of 1917 was bitter sweet. Alvin proposed to Theda the day he came home. She eagerly agreed. As their family and friends watched, on December 25, 1917, Alvin and Theda became husband and wife.

For Alvin and Theda, Allie and Norman, their time together was short and goodbyes seemed so final. After a scattering of desperate hugs and kisses, the men were gone.

For Alvin and Norman the waiting was over. They stepped from the boat onto French soil and the fight began. They knew full well there would be hardships, but they did not yet know the extent of those hardships.

Trenches were filled with disease, rodents and fallen soldiers.

World War I introduced trench warfare, and the condition in trenches were horrific. Death was a constant companion. Many novice soldiers were killed the first few days by mindlessly peering over the edge of walls into *no mans land*. There they would find the bullet of a sniper. It is estimated up to one-third of casualties occurred in the trenches.

A bullet or stray shrapnel wasn't the only thing soldiers worried about in the trenches. There were rats, hundreds and hundreds of them, attracted by the stench of unwashed bodies and death. Rats fed off the bodies of fallen soldiers who sometimes remained untouched for days or were hastily buried in shallow graves.

Rats, it seemed, were the only things well fed in the trenches. Some grew to the size of cats. During rare quiet times, soldiers would entertain themselves by clubbing, bayoneting or shooting the filthy creatures. As many rats as they killed, more would replace them.

It wasn't only the rats. Lice and nits were a constant problem. Breeding in the seams of filthy clothing, they couldn't be controlled and rapidly spread. Itching was sometimes so bad soldiers would scratch themselves raw. In addition to being a nuisance, lice caused the dreaded and deadly *trench fever*. This painful illness began with sudden, severe pain followed by high fever. Recovery away from the trenches took up to twelve weeks.

The trenches, in fact, were a breeding place for all sorts of disease-carrying bugs. Roaches, slugs, and horned beetles covered the walls making crusted dirt appear to move like a living creature. A man was expected to serve a trench duty rotation of seventy days or more. Those days seemed endless.

As if the constant gunfire, exploding bombs, vermin, bugs, and poisonous gases weren't enough to drive the soldiers insane, disease would. In 1918 a deadly illness spread. It started as a cough. Within a few hours the coughing would produce bleeding. Within days death would follow. The doctors were perplexed. They called it bloody pneumonia but knew it wasn't pneumonia. It would eventually be identified as the Spanish Flu. Tens of thousands of soldiers succumbed to the disease.

Alvin and Norman, second Lieutenants in the U.S. infantry, came face to face with all the ugliness of war. They did not falter, leading their men bravely into some of the war's most brutal battles. Mixing compassion with determination and dedication, they gained the respect of their platoons.

One of the greatest encounters of World War I occurred in Verdun, a northern town in France. It was one of the longest and fiercest battles of the war, causing mass casualties. While the main offensive ended in 1916, harsh battles continued until the end of the war.

Verdun, a major battlefield in World War I where thousands lost their lives.

In April of 1918, American forces were sent to Verdun to push back German armies who had recently gained ground. Norman and his platoon were part of that initiative.

During the battle, he led his men on a raid against the Germans. The battle was fierce. In the end, Norman and his men were victorious. The Germans were driven back and the Allies had regained ground.

The troops were jubilant, but Norman's triumph was clouded by the knowledge that many very brave men had fallen. Letters would be written to families but, no matter what was said, it would not be enough. Perhaps at that moment he thought of his own family, his brother Daniel who was an officer in training at the Aero Squadron, and, of course, Allie.

The men were returning from the raid when the threatening whistle of an incoming shell was heard. Norman, very familiar with the sound, quickly turned. It took him only a fraction of a second to realize it was too late. The shell burst. Shards of twisted shrapnel slammed into his body. Norman was down. It was bad, very bad, but he was still alive. Medics rushed him to the field hospital but nothing could save him. His life was gone as were his hopes and dreams. Were his last thoughts of Allie and his family? We will never know.

It was April and a beautiful spring day in Mecosta County. Allie was eagerly counting her final days of high school and anticipating another summer. She had been relatively happy that day. News on the war was good. People were saying the Allies were winning and the war might soon be over. She could hardly wait to see her brother again and, of course, Norman.

Coming home she called for her mother. When she didn't respond, Allie went in search and wandered into the kitchen. There she found her mother sitting at the table with Norman's mother, who was weeping. Allie halted in her steps. She knew what had happened.

The fighting continued overseas. Alvin had battled through some of the fiercest offensives and survived. He wrote to his devoted Theda and loving family almost daily. Their return letters helped get him through the horrors he had seen. Theda and his family reminded him what he was fighting for.

The Germans were not fairing well in their efforts. The fact was they were losing the war. German leaders believed they could turn it around with a decisive victory in Belgium, specifically Flanders. As a diversionary tactic, they sent German forces to Marne, France.

On July 15, 1918, the last major offensive of World War I began. It would be known as the Second Battle of the Marne.

The Germans attacked French forces with a powerful blow. The French called in more forces including over 85,000 U.S. soldiers. Alvin's platoon was part of that U.S. offensive.

Fighting was brutal, non-stop for three days and three nights. It is said the hardships and horrors the soldiers experienced in this battle could never be fully described or understood. It could only be experienced.

July 18, French and U.S. forces were joined by the British and Italians as the major counter-offensive began. Massive amounts of soldiers on foot and horseback collided. The pounding of horse hooves mingled with their fearful whinnies as riders drove them toward danger.

Tanks relentlessly rolled across the field over bodies of the fallen and through bombed-out craters. From their turrets, gunners fired continuous rounds. Exploding bombs merged with the cries and moans of the wounded and dying.

Pershing led troops in the bloody Second Battle of the Marne.

One of the major counter-offensives during the Second Battle of the Marne was a secretly planned attack that would take place at Château-Thierry. It was one of the first battles led by the Americans under the leadership of General John "Black Jack" Pershing.

In the early morning hours of July 18, under the cover of darkness, U.S. forces along with French forces and some colonials, quietly moved behind enemy lines. Unsuspecting Germans were taken by complete surprise when American and allied forces suddenly went "Over the Top." The battle was fierce. In the years that followed, surviving German soldiers would describe the American units as "fearless" and "relentless," especially considering they were behind enemy lines.

This nightmarish, deafening cacophony of battle continued until July 20 when the Allies finally drove German forces back, and the Second Battle of the Marne was over.

It was on July 18, 1918, during the Battle of Château-Thierry, Second Lieutenant Alvin Holen fell as he led his men forward. Alvin was one of 67,000 casualties in this operation. There were more than 288,000 casualties in the Second Battle of the Marne.

Alvin Holen lost his life during a counter offensive at Battle of Château-Thierry during the Second Battle of the Marne.

Just four months after Alvin's death, on November 11, 1918, a truce was declared. The war was essentially over. The Allies were victorious and democracy was preserved. Second Lieutenants Alvin Holen and Norman Hood, though not around to celebrate this great victory, would remain forever alive and respected as two of America's great fallen heroes.

Lieutenant Norman Hood's body eventually made its way back home. Alvin's body did not. Due to the massive deaths in the battlefield at Marne, Alvin, along with thousands of other soldiers, was interred at the site of the battle.

How do you describe profound grief? It is an endless sense of hopelessness, a feeling that life has no meaning. No future worth living. Everything important is gone. Gone. That is what Theda felt after the death of her beloved Alvin. That is what the Hood family and Holen families felt. And that, most certainly, is what Allie felt. She was too young to carry such a heavy, emotional burden. Was the loss of her brother just three months after the death of Norman too much for her to bear?

On a warm summer day, just a few weeks after the family received notice of Alvin's death, Allie went to Townline Lake. It was near 5:00 p.m. She stood away from the other folks enjoying the water. According to reports, she remained there for a time then jumped in and did not come up. It took 30 minutes before they found her body. Death records called it an accident. Perhaps it was.

Allie walked into the lake and drowned.

Chistena, being a strong, determined woman, pulled herself together for the sake of her remaining children. However, memories of her once happy life on the farm drove her away. She moved from Colfax and Townline Lake never to return.

For just a few short, impossibly perfect weeks as Alvin's bride, Theda had been given a glimpse into what a future for the two of them would have been... beautiful, loving, joyful. Those memories remained until her last breath. Alvin was and would always remain the greatest man she'd ever known and her only husband. Although she had several admirers, she never remarried telling each of them she was already married.

After Alvin's death, Theda continued her education and graduated with a Bachelor of Arts Degree from the University of Michigan. For several years she managed a woman's boarding home at the university. At one point she served as a servant for a wealthy business retailer eventually taking a position at the Liggett School in Detroit. Theda lived frugally, saving her money with one dream in mind.

Finally, in 1930, that dream came true. She withdrew her savings and purchased a single ticket on a ship destined for France and the Village of Belleau. Her journey ended at the foothills of Belleau Woods. How different it must have looked then compared to what her husband had seen some twelve years before. Now the scene was stunningly beautiful—a lush sweeping landscape surrounded by rolling hills. The last place her husband had been and still was. Now, at last, they shared this view together.

Alvin is just one of the thousands buried in this French cemetery.

She wandered the memorial park grounds. Shell holes, trenches and remnants of weapons could still be seen on the battle site. Eventually she made her way through the rows of more than 2,000 tombstones representing the fallen U.S. soldiers finally stopping at the one she had traveled thousands of miles to see. It was a simple cross with the engraved name, Second Lieutenant Alvin Holen. What she thought or said to her love during that time will always remain between Theda and Alvin.

As night descended, with visitors gone, the memorial park grew silent. Endless rows of tombstones cast their dark shadows across the hallowed ground. Beneath one, the stone engraved with the name Second Lieutenant Alvin Holen, a single rose lay.

Theda lived to the age of seventy-one. She quietly passed away at a nursing home in Detroit.

It took months for us to complete this remarkable story, a story that became much more than a ghost story. We returned to the lake on several occasions as the months of our research progressed. Though we never did see the ghostly vision of the Lady of the Lake, there were a few EVPs captured.

Before submitting this story to our publisher, we headed back to Townline Lake one last time with a plan in mind. There needed to be closure. We took our audio recorder and stood out on the dock. Although to be perfectly honest we felt a little foolish talking to an open lake, that's exactly what we did.

We called to Allie and Norman, Theda and Alvin explaining we were about to publish their story. They would not be forgotten.

We said that if any of them remained at the lake it was now time to move on. Their loved ones were waiting for them. Before leaving, we tossed a single rose into the lake's clear waters. It floated for some time until a gentle wave, like an eager hand, tossed it around and took it down and out of our sight.

It was during this session our last EVP was recorded. Just two words, "... cannot stay." Were the words residual? Did they capture a moment in time? Perhaps it was the response of Norman or Alvin to their lovers' plea not to leave.

We hoped the EVP was an acknowledgement to what we'd said. They now understood it was time to move on and they could no longer stay. We want to believe it was the latter. That would mean this tragic story has a happy ending.

Story Three:
Cottonwood B&B

9583 W. Front Street,
Empire, Michigan 49630
231-326-5535

Password: eagle146

Guest Investigator:
Tammy Schuster, Psychic Medium

THIS IS AN UNUSUAL TALE, but then it was an unusual investigation. Looking into the circumstances and events, it seems to be a ghost story within a ghost story.

Nestled in the majestic Sleeping Bear Sand Dunes lays the quiet Village of Empire with about 400 permanent residents. Not much bad news comes out of Empire.

Cottonwood Bed and Breakfast is just a couple of blocks from the center of town. Holly and Judy Decker, daughter and mother, own this charming B&B. They named it Cottonwood because of the beautiful cottonwood trees that shade the house and cover the grounds.

It is an inviting B&B in a peaceful town. Strangers driving by would never imagine the shroud of mystery that covers the home, but the town folks do. They remember all too clearly the strange and bizarre events that occurred not that many years ago.

The story revolves around the Roen family and the youngest sons that were raised, grew old, and died in the home. Well, at least two of them died in the home. No one really knows what happened to the third brother.

The family saga began in 1892 when Andrew Roen moved into the Empire area from Norway. Norway is a beautiful country known for spectacular skiing, abundant fishing, and enormous eagle populations. Norwegians are hard working folks, love the outdoors, and take great pride in their heritage.

There were no TVs in the late nineteenth century. As a close-knit family, Mom and Dad probably spent time talking about the homeland. Norwegians are known for their story telling. They told their children about their ancestors, Norwegian home, landscape, wild life and, of course, legends. It was a good family.

Empire was a perfect fit for Andrew. Back then the land was rugged, and to succeed you had to be a hard worker. He married a woman, Randi Holden, and they had seven sons: Alfred, Gilbert, Benhart, Sievert (died at birth), Sievert, Andrew and Reinhardt (died at birth).

It seemed a little strange to name their son Sievert after a son who just passed away. Maybe the name was important in the family, or the living boy was named to honor the dead. Regardless, Sievert was living in the shadow of his brother's spirit .

Randi and Andrew Roen were hardworking immigrants from Norway.

Original Roen family home

Hard working and frugal, the father labored at the sawmill in town, saved his money, and bought a bar in Empire that he would own until the 1930s. Around 1900 he purchased a house on a 133-acre farm and orchard in Empire.

Everyone knew and liked the Roens. Their sons were well respected in the village. The boys never caused problems; those called to active duty for WWI and WWII served honorably.

Roen boys from L to R: Alfred, Gilbert, Benhart, Sievert. Front: Andrew

Alfred and Gilbert, the oldest of the five boys would eventually marry and move out to start new lives with their families. Andrew Roen Sr. died in 1946, and ten years later his wife, Randi, passed away. Benhart, Sievert, and Andrew Roen continued living in the home.

Benhart was a teacher at the nearby school. As an educator he was well respected in the town. For years he planned lessons and activities for his students and ran a well-behaved and controlled classroom, Ben was a smart man, articulate, and the natural leader for his two younger brothers. He was a decisive, confident man used to planning and controlling his class and home.

Sievert tended the orchard, enjoying nature and the solitude of farming. A quiet man and a bit shy, he was known to stutter just a little when nervous or upset. Maybe that's why he enjoyed the orchards so much, they never made him nervous and never talked back. He was comfortable with his trees. He also enjoyed the independence farming offered. Sievert knew what needed to be done and enjoyed the freedom of not having a boss over his head.

The youngest brother, Andrew, loved cars and motorcycles. He was a mechanic in Empire and everyone liked him, especially if they owned a car or truck because he did good work. Andrew was fun loving, easy going, and enjoyed riding his motorcycle. As the youngest in the family, he was used to taking orders from his big brother Benhart, ten years his senior. The way Andrew saw it, if Ben said something it must be right because he was an educator.

Once their parents died, it was natural for Ben to run the homestead. He was the smart one and frequently made decisions independent of his brothers. Andrew didn't mind. That was just fine with him as long as he could work on his cars and ride the bike. He didn't care much for responsibility, and his big brother always seemed to know what to do.

Sievert was a different character. He was his own man in charge of the farm. When Ben's decisions or orders bothered Sievert, he would just go out and work the land. The orchard gave him an escape, a way to work out his frustrations.

Over time, as with all of us, the brothers retired, grew old and more reclusive. They didn't go into town as much, and most villagers didn't stop by to visit either. Many in town thought they were a little strange. Ben and Sievert were always arguing about one thing or another. Andy continued to tinker with cars and motorcycles.

There was a woman living with them. Possibly a boarder, but most thought she was Ben's girlfriend. A quiet life continued for the foursome.

With age, the three men were rarely seen and thought to be eccentric pack rats. They loved collecting antiques and never threw anything away.

Sievert moved away for a few years. It is believed he was in the Muskegon area, but no one knows for sure. He returned to live with his brothers around 1975. The arguments continued.

Sievert, now in his mid-seventies, was beginning to have problems remembering things. He would get confused and become easily upset, possibly a form of dementia. Ben had trouble dealing with that and their arguments became worse.

Occasionally Sievert would wander into town. He would tell anyone he saw his brothers, especially Ben, wanted to kill him.

Due to their strange behavior, family arguments, and increasingly reclusive nature, fewer and fewer people would stop by to say hello. Near the end, only two men came by: David Taghon and Gary Hilts. Dave and Gary enjoyed tinkering with engines and motorcycles, so they had a lot in common with Andrew. The three were friends.

We were privileged to be able to interview David Taghon. Dave owns and operates the Empire Area Museum right in the center of town.

Dave and Gary knew the brothers better than anyone. Dave recalled a day Sievert was walking in town holding a shotgun. Visibly upset, Sievert told Dave that Ben was going to kill him. Dave tried to reassure him.

On another occasion Dave told us about the time he took Sievert home. "I knocked on the door, and when Ben opened it and saw Sievert standing there, the sound of his voice went right through me. He loudly told him to get back to the orchard. Sievert was shaking."

Bickering continued between the brothers. Ben appeared to have an abnormal hatred for Sievert. He almost enjoyed bullying his brother. The arguing pitted Sievert against Ben. Andrew always took Ben's side. Sievert had no one.

By 1977, the fighting seemed to intensify. Folks just tolerated Sievert. They didn't really pay much attention to what he said. He was always afraid, whining about his brothers. Old, confused, and rambling on about this and that, people in town thought it was better to try and avoid Sievert.

It was a very hot night on July 30, 1977. There was a storm raging outside. With such bad weather, no one in his or her right mind would leave home. Best to stay inside. A person would have to be crazy to go out on a night like that.

After another one of their fierce arguments, according to Ben and Andrew, that is just what their crazy brother did. Sievert stomped out and slammed the door behind him. The seventy-five year old would never be seen again.

The town searched for days that turned into weeks, then months. Hundreds of police and volunteers scoured the woods and surrounding area. Even the local Boy Scouts joined in the search. There was no trace of the old man. The forest is very thick in and around Empire. When Kat and I were there, much of the forest had so much undergrowth we couldn't walk through it.

Many thought that in his mental state Sievert could have just wandered into the woods and gotten lost. If he made it far enough into the dense forest, it would be nearly impossible to find him. Some think he may have taken shelter under a tree and died from the elements.

Sievert's last few years at Cottonwood were lonely and, it seems, he lived in fear of his brothers. Is that how he died, alone and afraid?

Some believe Sievert might have gone as far as South Bar Lake. With the raging storm, an unsteady older man may have slipped, fallen in, and drowned. It's also possible a passing car picked up the old hitchhiker. He may have spent his last days in another town, his fate unknown.

According to several newspaper articles, the town doctor thought Sievert was still alive weeks after the search ended. However, considering the old man had no money and no means of support, you'd think someone would have found and reported him to the police. After all, his disappearance was in all the area newspapers. If he was in another town, it seems likely someone would have been able to trace him back to Empire. As it was, however, Sievert simply disappeared on that hot rainy night. He would soon become just another missing person in our state.

Yet there were whispers. Some in town remembered Sievert's fear of Ben. He would plead for their help without ever saying it directly. After all, Sievert knew Ben hated him, enjoyed tormenting him, and would one day kill him. That's what the crazy old man kept telling everyone. Until his disappearance, no one listened.

Maybe he wasn't as crazy as they thought. Maybe, in a heated argument, Ben did exactly what Sievert had predicted. Newspaper articles said that at least one man thought foul play was involved. That was their nephew, Jack Roen. Jack was suspicious because he had witnessed the extreme anger of their bickering.

Another reason to suspect foul play was mentioned by Dave Taghon. He began considering the possibility while reading Andrew's diary. Andy kept very meticulous notes in this book. One entry mentions that Andrew returned Sievert's Social Security check to the government the month after his disappearance.

The question becomes, why so soon? Sievert could have gone off planning, one day, to come back. Why not wait at least a few months before returning his Social Security checks? It seemed as if Andrew did not expect his brother to come back.

Dave said there really wasn't anything more to his suspicions than that. In the end, he did not think murder was the cause. Sievert just wandered off. Dave was a good friend to the brothers and may find it hard to think anything negative about them. Then again, maybe there was nothing negative or suspicious.

Yet rumors persisted. There were those who thought the body was buried on the grounds, in a septic field, or under parts of the home. Some also believe the body could be in a basement wall or under the cement floor. One psychic claimed the body of Sievert would be found in a cistern. Over the years, no matter what area was searched, his body was not discovered.

With no trace of Sievert, the town gradually returned to normal, and so did Ben and Andy. Life was peaceful.

Some years later, the local doctor was called because the woman living with Ben and Andy had not been seen in several days, and the brothers were worried. Again, many believe she was Ben's girlfriend. By that time in their lives, Ben was having trouble walking and getting around.

When the good doctor arrived, he found her dead in an upstairs room. She was ninety-two years old. The doctor considered her death to be natural.

Kat and I wonder why Andy didn't go upstairs to check on her. He was twelve years younger than Ben. Even though he had diabetes, Andy helped and took care of his big brother. He should have been able to climb the stairs. Also, Ben was suffering from a little dementia, but nothing indicates Andy had that problem. Why wait three days to notify someone? It just seems a little strange.

Well, the coroner's report claimed natural causes. There was never any type of serious investigation into her death, so it remains natural causes.

On a cold winter evening, January 17, 1985, the brothers' friend Gary Hilts called the house. No one answered. He waited until the next morning then called them again, but there was still no answer. That wasn't right. Gary became concerned and went to see Dave Taghon. They headed right over to the house.

As Dave explained to us, as soon as they opened the door the smell told them something was wrong. They immediately went into Andy's bedroom and found him lying dead in his bed.

Next they went looking for Ben and found him in the living room sitting in an upright position on the floor. Dead. Eerily, Ben's eyes were wide open, cold, and blank, a strange almost fearful expression on his face. His eyes were locked in a transfixcd stare at a stuffed bald eagle resting on the table.

Both brothers were gone. What happened? The coroner believes Andy died around January 10 with complications from diabetes. Stroke and heart attack are common for elderly diabetics. Andy kept meticulous records of his sugar levels in his diary. It appears Ben was trying to revive his brother. There was spilled orange juice on the bed. There was also rancid milk and stale crackers on the table.

Towards the end something seemed wrong. His diary entries were very shaky. Yet, Gary Hilts talked to him the week before and he seemed fine. Andrew's death was sudden and must have been from his sugar. What else could it be?

Ben died a few days later of natural causes, heart failure according to the coroner. Since Andy normally took care of him, maybe he hadn't eaten in a few days and it took its toll. Some newspaper accounts indicate that Ben could easily have died from grief over his younger brother's death or fear since Andy, his caregiver, was gone. That is all speculation. What else could it be?

Ben was found dead staring at the eagle

The funeral was very much like the last years of their lives. Ben and Andy were cremated with no ceremony or anyone in attendance. Gary Hilts received a call regarding the ashes. He took them to the cemetery. Gary dug a small hole in the ground and placed Andy inside. Ben was buried next to his girlfriend.

Some time later the Roen estate was divided up among two nieces and a nephew. There would be an auction to sell off much of the estate. Speculation was wild. Stories were being told of hidden money in the house and on the grounds as well as all sorts of valuable antiques including paintings, lamps, and tables.

Dave thinks that he and Gary found most of the cash when preparing for the sale. There was well over $100,000. He also told us about the rumors. Many were thinking that Sievert just might show up.

Labor Day weekend, 1985, the auction was held. Thousands attended from all over the country. Villager's eyes darted across the massive crowds looking for Sievert. He was nowhere to be seen. The auction was hugely successful raising hundreds of thousands.

There were many paintings, chests, tables, baby carriages to be sold along with antique lamps and more. Some came hoping to buy a piece that might have some of the hidden money reportedly still in the house. The historical society in town, The Heritage Group, would receive some of the items. Much is available in Dave Taghon's Empire Area Museum.

We had three brothers from a normal family and a normal background with such strange endings. Kat and I were really looking forward to this investigation. Joining us would be a long-time friend and well-known Michigan psychic, Tammy Schuster. We wondered what she might pick up and if she could help identify what happened to Sievert.

We packed our bags and drove north from Southeast Michigan on a chilly, rainy day in September. It was a long drive and Holly had offered us a room for the night. Upon our arrival we met up with Tammy. So, let's begin.

Cottonwood is a charming bed and breakfast, a great spot to spend the weekend if going to the Sleeping Bear Sand Dunes. The property is shaded with giant cottonwood trees. Inside, the home definitely embraces the past. Although the kitchen is very contemporary, the dining area and porch retain their historical ambiance. The dining room contains the original Roen stove. Not used today, it is a historical piece. On the wall, next to the old stove, is a small picture of the five brothers.

Judy greeted us with warmth and hospitality. Holly arrived shortly after. In just a few minutes we felt like old friends. Holly and her mother are doing major restoration to the B&B while keeping its earlier charm.

From L to R: Judy and Holly Decker host and manage Cottonwood

The Cottonwood room, pleasant and supposedly active.

We would be staying in one of the haunted bedrooms on the third floor, The Cottonwood. Comfortable, this was a large room with a queen and two twin beds. Hardwood floors took us back to an earlier time. Bed covers and furnishings were fresh and simple. Inviting and haunted, The Cottonwood was perfect for the night.

Holly claims a woman is often seen and heard in this room. Perfect. Maybe the boys' mother, Randi Roen, wanders the grounds or possibly grandma, Anne Holden.

Holly has never really experienced anything paranormal, but many guests disagree with her. Judy was more reserved when answering the question. She may have seen a few things but didn't elaborate.

Holly took us through the home to point out areas where people have had experiences and to go over some of the Roen history. There were a couple of bedrooms supposedly active on the second floor, with more activity in the dining area and first floor rooms. People experience footsteps, voices, and shadows when they stay.

When we arrived in the kitchen, we noticed the new, contemporary design. Holly explained the area was remodeled.

They had a fire recently and brought it all up to date during restoration.

The basement entrance is outside. When she brought our group downstairs, one of the first things mentioned was the cement patch. Not far from the entrance there was a section of cement that was definitely newer than the rest of the floor. It was approximately eight feet long and about four feet wide. In reality, that part of the floor was probably cut away for septic or plumbing repair. In the back of our minds, however, we remember the rumors that Sievert could be buried in the basement. Oh if we only had a jackhammer. That cement patch was the right size for a body.

Then she led us to the back and we noted a freezer. When asked what was in it, Holly didn't know. Neither she nor Judy had ever opened it. It had been there when they purchased the home. Approaching, we were immediately assaulted with a terrible odor, the kind that causes an involuntary gag reflex. We didn't open it at the time but knew it would have to be checked out later.

Freezer in the corner of the basement

That's the time she recommended we pay a visit to David Taghon, owner of the Empire Area Museum. The museum was closed, but Dave was kind enough to come over and give us a private tour. He was a fun and charming man. As mentioned before, Dave was one of the Roen brothers' friends. He is a wealth of knowledge regarding the town and anything related to the Roens.

Dave Taghon's museum is a great place to visit

The museum doesn't look that big on the outside, but it is remarkably large when you enter. The first floor is filled with a collection of artifacts and newspaper articles from the Roens that even includes part of the original bar Andrew Sr. owned and an old record player plus so much more.

One item that stood out was a large brown eagle with wings stretched out and fierce, intimidating, piercing eyes. Dave told us how he found Ben staring at that bird when his body was discovered.

Downstairs was just as fascinating with little historic shops set up from the 1800s and 1900s. It was obvious he had spent a lot of time developing the museum, which is really remarkable. Anyone visiting Empire should without question include the museum as part of their visit. Naturally they should stay at the Cottonwood B&B.

Upon our return to Cottonwood, Holly and Judy said good night. It was time to begin. Our investigation would focus on the first and second floors as well as the basement. With luck we would spend the evening with three charming men, Benhart, Andrew and Sievert.

The first stop was the second floor. This visit, nothing seemed to happen, but we would be back several times during the evening.

Descending to the dining room and kitchen area Kat saw the K2 going crazy and, at the same time, thought there was a shadow. Tammy had also seen a shadow and sensed a spirit moving through the walls. It must have moved to another room because the K2 stopped reacting.

We were getting ready to move to the basement. Kat and Tammy were talking about being cold. They stopped, looked at me and thought something was wrong. My face was red and I was sweating.

Tammy said, "How could you be hot in here?"

Kat added, "I am freezing."

In truth, I didn't feel unusually warm or uncomfortable. I felt just great. Still, I rinsed my face with cold water. That was strange, but then this would be a strange evening for all of us.

Packing up our gear, we started for the basement when Tammy, once again, became freezing cold. At that moment the K2 began to hit again. Kat checked the surroundings. EMF levels were naturally high. We suspected electrical wiring may have caused the EMF and K2 reaction but there was no explanation for Tammy's chills.

Finally making it to the basement, we propped the door open. I have seen enough scary movies to know that people are always getting locked in the basement with monsters. We were not going to fall victim to that.

Once downstairs, we got our bearings and headed over to check the freezer. It looked like something from maybe the 1950s or 60s. I opened the lid and we all peered into the dark hole. We were immediately assaulted with a strong, acidic, nauseating odor. Horrible!

What we saw inside was unrecognizable. Whatever it had been, it was nothing but a mush of mold and decay, possibly even black mold. It was really hard to say.

The odor was unbearable. Something was definitely rotting. It burned our nostrils as we inhaled. What was it? I took a couple of pictures and quickly closed the lid.

Next, our little group walked over to the fresher patch of cement Holly showed us earlier. We thought it would be wise to hold an EVP session in this area. If, that is, the terrible odor than now filled the basement would allow us to stay downstairs long enough. The effects of the pungent smell from the freezer was taking a toll on us.

During our brief questioning not much happened. We were all having just a little trouble breathing. Our time was cut short, but we would be back.

Once outside, a break was in order. It was a relief to breathe in some fresh air. Kat and Tammy were actually nauseous from the unbelievable stench. None of us will ever forget that putrid odor.

Returning to the dining area, I began to look at the basement pictures. Something caught my eye in one of the photos of the freezer interior. Enlarging it I saw something I couldn't explain. It was a face. Just then the K2 on the table next to me went crazy. I turned the camera off. The K2 stopped. I thought my camera may have triggered the instrument.

I turned the camera back on and the K2 didn't react. Even as I continued going through the photos, the K2 remained flat. It wasn't until I reached the picture of the freezer that it went off again. The face was clearly just a matrix. Having taken thousands of pictures during investigations I knew it was a matrix, but it looked eerily familiar.

Going to the wall and examining the picture of the Roen brothers, there it was. The image my camera picked up looked very much like Sievert. The face was long and thin with a long, thin nose. This was crazy!

Sitting at the table again, I was trying to explain it to myself when Tammy came over. At this point the K2 was flat. I told her about the photo. She asked to see it. I pushed my preview button and flipped through the shots taken. When I reached that one picture the K2 reacted again. Tammy looked at the photo quickly seeing the image. We went back to the wall photo showing the picture of the brothers, Sievert amongst them. Holding the camera next to the photo was startling. Yup that was Sievert.

To the right of the Styrofoam cup debris that matrixed into a face similar
in shape to Sievert. Did he want us to know he was there that night?

Tammy is a great psychic and has also been on numerous
investigations. She knows a matrix when she sees one and agreed
with me. It was indeed a matrix. Perhaps a bizarre coincidence
that it looked like Sievert but still a matrix. All the while, the K2
lights are wildly flashing. I flipped to another photo and the K2
stopped.

Kat entered the room wondering what we were doing. Again
I repeated the story and showed her the photo and again the K2
reacted. So now the three of us went back to the wall and huddled
around the picture hanging there. I put the camera up to it and
everyone agreed, Sievert.

We stood there transfixed for several minutes. If Sievert was watching, he probably thought we were three weird women. Well, we are, but that evening we were weirder than normal. As the night went on, my camera never impacted the K2 unless I turned to that one picture. No matter where I was, the K2 would just go crazy.

A little later, inside the dining area, Kat and Tammy were still talking about the pungent smell from the freezer when the K2 again became active. Thinking it may be Sievert needing to get our attention, Kat asks him to back away, calm down so we could help. The lights kept flashing. We would later discover, at that moment, a very soft voice was recorded. "That's not right."

Tammy felt the energy with us was angry and confused, and that's why the K2 was reacting so wildly. Kat asked, "Are you Sievert?"

It was then our recorder picked up an incredible response. A distant whisper, "Yes I am Sievert."

Several questions later Tammy asked if he wanted closure, "Do you just want to be found?" The answer, "Yes."

"Are you angry, Sievert? Are you afraid, Sievert?" A soft yes was recorded to both responses.

Kat continued, wanting to know if it was Sievert's face in the freezer. Although nothing was recorded on audio, Tammy picked up on his thoughts. She said it was his energy. He wanted us to know he was here.

Then there seemed to be a noise, an undefinable rap in a back, first floor bedroom. We quickly entered. Everything was in order and quiet.

Throughout the evening, noises and knocks were heard from different rooms. Whenever we approached the area of the sound, it would stop. It continued throughout the night and was frustrating. Up and down the stairs all night long, following the noises but never catching anything. If the spirits were trying to wear us out, it was working.

At one point, Kat and Tammy were in the middle bedroom on the second floor running an EVP session. The room itself is a pretty room, cozy with the bed full of dolls. Although deceivingly pretty, it is said to be haunted by a woman, possibly the boarder who is believed to have passed away here. There are some who also believe the spirit of a little girl also remains. Who the little girl might be is unknown. During their first session no evidence was recorded.

When they left, however, Kat placed an audio recorder on a table. It remained there for two hours and, during that time, several EVPs were collected. The first was recorded when Kat returned to the room, about twenty minutes after leaving. She walked in and cheerfully said, "Hello, my name is Kathleen. Can you tell me your name please?" A male voice called out, "Here, I am in here." It could also be, "Help, I am in here."

While we were in the second floor hallway, Tammy thought she heard a voice. Shortly after she made that claim, the recorder in the room captured another EVP. "I built this house." The Roen father, Andrew built the home. Was it he who responded? It is entirely possible many of the family still remain at Cottonwood.

Just a few minutes later, in the same room, a female voice was picked up, "Sweetheart." It sounded like the voice of a loving mother. Perhaps it was Randi calling to one of her young sons or maybe Ben's girlfriend calling to him. There were a few more significant EVPs captured in that area. They will be explained later.

The Roen boys' grandmother, Anna Holden, died at Cottonwood in 1925. She was Randi's mother and had a first floor room. Walking into the room that was once hers was very pleasant, relaxing. Before the first question was even asked, however, a disembodied voice was picked up. Actually, it sounds like a young male spirit, maybe a teenager, "They're coming." It almost sounded as if he was warning someone of our arrival.

I've always wondered, when people pass on at what age do they return? Is it possible they come back at a time in their lives when they were the most comfortable or the most tormented? Possibly young Andy or one of the other brothers enjoyed their teen years and returned as a young man.

Tammy was sensing activity in a number of rooms.

Moving upstairs again we continued investigating each room. At one point Tammy's battery died. Her camera was giving her problems that day. It would turn on then off for no apparent reason all night long, and now the battery was dead.

We went downstairs where I had fresh batteries to give Tammy. In the past, Kat and I have bought batteries and the package was defective. That could have been Tammy's problem.

Once her camera was working, Tammy wanted to go down in the basement again. There was no way I was going back to that foul-smelling place, so I smiled and told her to go. She looked at me wide-eyed, "You want me to go alone!"

I laughed and said, "Yes, I do. You already knew that? Wow, you're a really good psychic!" Tammy gave a hearty laugh and dismissively waved her hand at me.

She decided to stay with us as we moved into the living room. This was the room where Ben died sitting in an upright position against the wall, his fearful eyes frozen on the eagle.

Kat directed questions at Ben. When she asked if he was happy when Andy died, we saw the K2 immediately light up. Following, a quiet whisper was recorded, "No."

We think Ben and Andy were very close. One year they shared a memorable trip to Europe. They often spoke about the great time they had. As they grew older, they became even closer, caring for one another.

A few minutes later Tammy asked if the spirit was giving her a headache. A faint knock was picked up on audio. Kat asked if Andy was here and another faint knock could be heard.

Returning to the kitchen, we wanted to see if the K2 would again react to that picture in my camera. Sure enough, almost on cue, when we brought it up to the picture on the wall, the K2 simply went crazy.

We decided it was time to take a coffee break. This was a fairly eventful evening. Kat, Tammy, and I needed to calm down as much as Sievert.

During this time, the three of us continued talking to Sievert and staring at the photo I had taken earlier. I was certain it was a matrix image and not the real spirit of Sievert, and yet I couldn't look away. It almost looked like the matrix face was grinning. At one point I asked if he was smiling.

Kat said, "Is that a grimace?"

I followed, "Are you in pain?" An EVP followed, "Yes."

Several times while in the kitchen we asked Sievert how he died and who killed him. If he was there, he chose not to answer.

Kat asked Sievert to communicate and come to the black box on the table near me. Kat, referring to me said, "Tell us what you want her to do." Again, a whisper, "Nothing."

We continued to talk to him over our coffee break, and each time, the K2 responded. Tammy sensed that he wanted us to go back to the basement. Well, to be honest, that was really the last place I wanted to be, but this time I was out voted. It looked like after the coffee break we were headed to the dreadful basement. When the decision to return was made, the K2 went flat. He seemed to be gone.

We were all really charged. This had been an unusual experience. The remarkably consistent K2 responses certainly suggested our company for the evening was Sievert. What we would later discover is that audio evidence would support all three brothers were likely with us that evening.

Most investigations are very uneventful. Tonight was not the case. There was plenty going on to keep us wide-awake.

During our coffee break, Tammy sensed that Sievert liked me, claiming I reminded him of his mother. Well, isn't that special. Tammy felt he was shy around me and didn't handle flattery and compliments well. That's why the K2 would go full red at times because he would be nervous or agitated over our comments.

Our conversation continued. Tammy said that Sievert had a crush on me. Oh great, I thought. Kat chuckled, "That's just your freakin' luck."

Well, you take what you can get I always say. Good to know a guy in a black-mold freezer loves me. Tammy agreed saying dead, black-mold men tend to like me.

I glanced at Kat and said, "Next investigation, no psychic!"

We laughed and continued idle chatter. What we were really doing was stalling the inevitable. None of us wanted to go back to the basement though we knew we must.

Eventually packing our equipment, the downstairs investigation started. This time we took wash cloths to cover our faces to protect ourselves from the smell. It really was intolerable down there.

Going directly to the freezer, we reluctantly opened the lid. Looking down Tammy and Kat saw an object about two inches wide and maybe six inches long. They thought it looked like a bone. More than likely it was a stick or pipe.

We started an EVP session. Questions began with Kat, "Sievert, please talk to us. We're here. Communicate in some way with us. You wanted us down here."

It was then a very soft voice was recorded, "I am not Sievert."

This was a surprise. If not Sievert, then who? Everything to this point indicated we were talking to him. This EVP suggested someone else, possibly Ben or Andy?

Again Kat asked, "Sievert, where are you, sir?" A reply, "Right here."

L to R Tammy and Kat covering their faces because
of the odor, while they seriously investigate.

Now the question becomes was it Sievert responding or not. Kat continued, "We just want to be sure we got your message right. You wanted us down here, but for what purpose?" Another EVP, this one was more difficult to understand, but it sounded like "Here Ben." Or "Here now."

Both Kat and Tammy started getting headaches. We knew time was limited and the air down here not healthy. Almost simultaneously, each of us saw shadows in different areas of the basement. Three separate shadows seen by each of us. The three brothers?

Unfortunately, it was not recorded and is not considered evidence, just a personal experience. Of course, we had to consider the likelihood the foul odor had affected our judgment. Yet, it was still curious that each of us saw separate shadows at the same time.

Back in the kitchen we checked photos and video. It was strange the shadows appeared at same time, but nothing was captured. There were only a few lights on in the basement. It's possible the shadows were merely a trick of the eye caused by the dim lighting.

As we were reviewing our cameras, there was a noise like a rattle. Tammy said, "I didn't do that. It rattled all by itself, like someone kicked my bench." Kat remembered that she too had felt her chair move earlier in the evening.

A noise, similar to the first, came again. It sounded like a knock or rattle. Kat asked for the sound to be repeated. A few minutes later, it was. In fact, it occurred twice more on request. We sat there for several minutes in silence and listened. The sound continued sporadically. We decided it was likely the natural creaking of the old home.

We went back to examining the photos. Looking at the contents of the freezer, we could see a plastic cup, a long thin object, and something bizarre. It almost looked like a jaw bone. It was too hard to tell. Even today looking at the photo it is really hard to know what you are looking at in all that decay. More than likely it was rotted food and debris. None of us were going back down there to examine it.

Discussing the events of the evening, we agreed what we were dealing with was an intelligent haunting. Sitting at the table, Kat brought up an interesting point, "You know what I am beginning to wonder, perhaps he wanted us in the basement because something was going on up here."

Tammy, "Could be, but we had cameras and audio up here also."

I replied, "But not in this room, and this is where he was the most active."

Kat, "What was going on in the kitchen that he would want us out of this room?" It could have been any family member or even someone unconnected with the family trying to get us out. Were we getting over zealous, putting way too much into it? I don't know, but it was a curious thought.

At this point the K2s were completely dead, unresponsive for some time. It was one of the first times that evening we felt completely alone. Had the spirits finally left?

It seemed that most of what happened during the investigation was in the kitchen. Tammy thought this area could be the center of activity and, for some reason, the spirits wanted us out. Again EMF levels were checked. This time we checked the stove and, to our surprise, discovered unusually high EMF levels around it.

The stove hadn't operational for a long time. Some metals do seem to hold high EMF levels. Could that be the cause, or might it be something else?

The stove was the only thing left from the Roens. That brings up the possibility that spirits can attach to an object. If not directly connected, they may stay close to something from their past, something familiar. Is that what had happened here?

The investigation was coming to an end. It had been a very long night. About 2:30 a.m. Tammy went home. Kat and I headed to our room.

The stove is the only item original to the Roen family.
Can it draw the spirit of those that have passed on?

Kat naturally grabbed the large bed before I got in, leaving me with a double. She was laughing about it, but that's okay because I loved my bed, tall with a great mattress. Kat, being a little shorter than me, got a bed that was even taller than mine. First time getting in bed she literally had to jump and throw herself across the mattress. My bed had a stepping stool to use, which I didn't need. Should I tell Kat about the stool? I didn't think so. Now it was my turn to laugh.

Before drifting off, we left audio and video running throughout the night hoping to capture evidence that would point to the presence of the boys' mother, grandmother, or Ben's girlfriend. As it turned out, it was a very peaceful night and nothing was recorded.

Naturally with Sievert missing, a main focus of the investigation was to find out as much as possible about his disappearance and determine who remained at the home. We took the audio evidence recorded and combined those with the facts known about the family. From that we put together a scenario, like a game of Clue. What might have happened?

On that dark, stormy night in July 1977, Ben and Sievert were fighting again. By all accounts, it was intense. Based on some of the EVPs collected, we believe bits and pieces of that violent argument were captured.

Our audio recorder picked up several voices. The first was, "Here, I am in here." Or "Help, I am here." It was coming from a second floor bedroom. Was it Sievert calling for help? We know Sievert was afraid of his older brother. We also know, when it came to Sievert, Ben had a short temper. About an hour later the voice, "They hate me," was recorded followed by, "Die."

Next, Ben came upstairs looking for Sievert. Andy followed calling out his name, "Ben." When he finally found his brother, Ben told Sievert just what he was going to do to him. Sievert would die.

How did Sievert die, and did Ben actually kill him? Perhaps the answers to those questions would be discovered in the audio collected at the kitchen table. On many occasions the K2 was directly reacting to questions. During that time, several relevant EVPs were captured.

Tammy wanted to know if he was angry, afraid. The recorded response was "Yes" to both questions. I wanted to know if he was in pain. The EVP said, "yes."

Finally, a simple question from Kat, "How did you die, Sievert." And a simple answer from Sievert, "Ben hit me." That's all there is to it.

It seems all three brothers remain at Cottonwood along with other family. Perhaps they are attached to the last object in the home that was theirs, the stove.

Now, what about the mysterious deaths of Ben and Andy? Yes, the coroner said they both died from natural causes. Indeed, it very likely was natural. Certainly, a heart attack is natural. But could something have happened to trigger the fatal heart attack? Can a person be scared to death?

It is possible Sievert did return to Cottonwood? Not in body but in spirit?

Did he come back to exact his revenge? Often a person can wait an eternity for retribution. Is that what happened?

Ben died staring, wide eyed and in fear, at the eagle in the living room. We wondered if there was any significance to that eagle.

Further research turned up some interesting facts. Around the world the eagle represents justice, strength and spirituality. It transcends the earth and reaches the heavens. In the Roen's homeland, Norway, mythology tells of the Blood Eagle, a form of torture and death, a legend that passes on through the generations. Had their father ever shared that story with his sons? The last thing Ben saw was the eagle glaring down at him.

Did Sievert return to Cottonwood? What caused Ben's death? Perhaps the secret lies with the eagle.

Story Four:
Hotel Montcalm B&B

106 S. Camburn
Stanton, MI 48888
989-831-5055
Guest Investigator: Dawn James

Password: amu14

WHO IS FRED? THE UNCLE your mother says never to mention?
Well, maybe, but for this story it was the name of the town
created as the county seat for Montcalm County. The town was
named in 1840 after Fred Hall, the original landowner. In 1862
the town's name changed to Stanton.

The Hotel Montcalm has been a part of Stanton for over 150
years. People have come and gone. Do some of their stories remain
locked within the rooms of this hotel? The evidence collected
during our investigations led to both gripping and completely
unexpected discoveries.

Hotel Montcalm at the turn of the century

We go back to the tale of Amanda and Frank Upright.

Amanda Upright's youth is a mystery. Few records were found
of her existence until the tragic events of March 19, 1881. Not
even her name is certain.

One record indicates she was born Mabel (Amanda) Stevens
around 1863. According to Amanda's story, at the age of fourteen
she was forced into marrying Franklin Upright. An abusive man,
a drifter, Frank never stayed in one place very long. The thing he
was best at was tormenting his young and inexperienced bride.

What is curious is that neither census records nor old city

directories showed her living with Frank. Their relationship was, at best, ambiguous.

According to newspaper reports, Frank worked in a lumber camp outside of Stanton. On Saturday, March 19, 1881, he went to the hotel where his wife was staying. Loud voices were heard coming from her room.

Frank threatened to kill Amanda. She pleaded for her life. After he left, Amanda ran from her room, terrified, and hid in another.

Time passed and when she felt safe, Amanda left the building through a side entrance. Frank was waiting outside and quickly followed her down Main Street, eventually overtaking her. According to records, she was heard pleading for her life, "Oh don't shoot me." It spite of her pleas he stepped up and, point blank, emptied his revolver. Two shots struck her head, the rest, her body.

Main Street looking East from Court Street, Stanton, Mich.

Frank chased Amanda down this road, Main Street, and shot her.

Leaving his wife lying bleeding in the snow, Frank casually strolled to a saloon. He ordered some hard cider and calmly waited for the police. Later, he told a news reporter that every shot took effect and was reported saying, "I meant to kill her and I did. I am ready to die for it."

People went rushing to Amanda. To their amazement, she was still alive. Frank was immediately arrested. He justified his actions by saying she had been criminally intimate with other men. He shot Amanda in the heat of passion.

Amanda lingered for fifteen days, floating in and out of consciousness. During her lucid moments, she told police what had happened. From that they built a scenario of the events leading up to the shooting. A March 21, 1881, article in the *Detroit Free Press* told her story.

Amanda claimed her marriage to Frank was brutal. For a long time he demanded she "part with her virtue to get money for him," but she continued to refuse. Then, two months prior to the shooting, she relented when his threats became more violent.

As Amanda's story continued, she stated that during the two-month period she had given her husband over $200. On Friday, March 18, her husband demanded another $25 by the next day or he would kill her.

Saturday afternoon, he came to the Stanton Hotel demanding the money. She didn't have it. Amanda pleaded for him to wait until Sunday. Frank would not. She told the police if she had had the money, Frank would not have hurt her. Adding to the irony, the $1.45 pistol he purchased that day came from the money she had given him.

To make matters worse, in the days following the shooting, Amanda contracted measles. She finally gave up her life on April 3, 1881. She was not yet eighteen years old.

Frank Upright was tried in Stanton. After two days the jury found him guilty of first degree murder. From the beginning he claimed the trial wasn't fair. He didn't have an attorney until the day he went to court. Adding to his protests, he had wanted a man by the name of Charles Chilson to be subpoenaed, and his attorney refused. According to Frank, Chilson had offered to pay him money for the "wrong that had been done to him."

None of this ultimately mattered to the court. He was sentenced to life in solitary confinement at the notoriously cruel Jackson Prison. Frank would spend the next 30 years living at Jackson. When released in 1911, he would have the distinction of being the longest serving prisoner at Jackson.

Frank was found guilty of murdering his wife and sentenced to
life in solitary confinement at the brutal Jackson State Prison

What is the real story behind Frank and Amanda Uprights'
lives that led to her murder? Was her final statement true or her
last act of revenge against a cruel, unloving husband? The truth
remains with Frank and Amanda.

The story of Frank and Amanda had long been forgotten until
our research uncovered it shortly before our first investigation at
the hotel.

We learned about Hotel Montcalm B&B through one of our
paranormal contacts, Scott. Based on his experiences and evidence,
he believed the hotel to be haunted.

It was a bitterly cold January night when Kat and I met with
fellow investigator Dawn James. Deep piles of snow lined the
deserted streets of Stanton. A chill clung to us as we entered the
warmth and subdued lighting of the inn.

Although Kat and I are not usually sensitive, we can honestly
say there was something in the atmosphere of this historic hotel that
filled us with anticipation. Dawn, who has some level of sensitivity,

stopped at the hotel's entrance. Her eyes quickly darted around. All she said was "Wow." Kat asked "Are you getting something already?" Dawn nodded her head and simply said, "Yes."

As in any investigation where we work with a sensitive, the history and haunting of a location is not shared. This is done to ensure their *impressions or feelings* during their walk-through aren't influenced. Such was the case with Dawn. To this point she knew little about the hotel, other than it was historic and located in Stanton, Michigan.

Scott greeted us then introduced us to the hotel owner, Judy Guevara, and her sister. During our conversation, Dawn wandered into a back room, avoiding our conversation.

Judy told us that she had never personally experienced anything unusual although numerous family, friends, and guests had. Others have heard voices and footsteps and have seen fleeting apparitions. Some people will not stay the night in room six, on the second floor. At least one report claims the bed moved, and others mention voices or just an uncomfortable feeling.

Judy Guevara talks about the B&B's history

After our meeting, we went looking for Dawn and found her in the antiques shop. She turned to Kat but appeared lost in thought.

L to R Bev and Dawn. Dawn sensed more than one male presence
and a woman in the gift shop during the investigation.

"I just got chills," she said.

Kat asked if it was related to the antique jewelry, possibly an
attachment to the shop items. Dawn didn't think so. She felt the
strong presence of a man with a pocket watch. Following her
feeling, she walked into the hallway and sensed a lady.

She pointed to a corner and said, "Here, there is a lady right
here. She has an apron on. She was one of the workers."

Kat walked to that area and asked if the lady was with her.
Half laughing Kat said, "I don't feel anything." Neither Dawn
nor Kat knew at the time but, at that moment, the first EVP was
captured. A whispered voice, "Some people don't see."

Some people don't see, the possible meaning of those words was
intriguing. What exists around us that our eyes do not see? Most
psychics or sensitives claim to see or hear things the rest of us
do not. Are there really people who have what some call a *Third
Eye?* These individuals have different visual perceptions beyond
our own. Are they really able to reach into other dimensions, other
realms and see what we do not. *Some people don't see.*

Trying to understand and validate the many theories in the paranormal community is what drives us to continue our research and explore possibilities. The paranormal field has no black and white answers. It would be less frustrating if it did.

After walking through the first floor, we ascended to the second where the guest rooms are located. We found nicely appointed rooms on either side of a spacious lounge area that includes a pool table—a great place for guests to relax and socialize.

Our first stop would be Room 1. Scott told us about an incident that occurred here. A woman spending the night left her rings on the table. The next morning when she awoke they were gone, but the door to her room was locked. They were never found.

While Scott was talking Kat noticed a pensive look on Dawn's face. "Do you feel something?"

Dawn replied, "The next room over."

They moved into Room 2; Kat questioned, "What do you feel?"

"Sexual tension," Dawn said. She sensed it was one woman's room but men were involved. There was resentment and conflict. She believed there were illicit relationships in this room. Scott and I entered overhearing the conversation. He pointed to the bed and said some women felt the bed move when they laid on it.

Our group slowly moved through the other rooms. In the hallway approaching Rooms 5 and 6 Dawn paused. She was picking up a name. She thought for a moment then told us she was picking up a name that began with a "Ch..." like Charles. She wasn't certain, however if the Ch was the beginning of a first name or last name.

We had not shared the story of Frank and Amanda Upright with Dawn. In fact, at this point, neither Kat nor I even knew about Charles Chilson and his important connection to Amanda Upright. If what Frank believed was true, Charles Chilson frequently visited Amanda at the hotel.

We walked into Room 6 and Dawn abruptly halted. Overwhelmed with a sudden, profound sorrow, she almost immediately turned to leave. She put up a hand as if to push away the negative energy and said, "No, I can't. I want to cry."

Strong emotions were felt in the second floor rooms, especially Room 6.

This may have been the room where Amanda hid
trying to avoid the anger of her husband.

Kat questioned, "It makes you want to cry?"

I looked at Dawn and her response was obvious from the tears welling in her eyes.

Kat, "Do you think something bad happened?

Dawn gave an affirmative response, but didn't know if it was a death or not. It was just very negative, emotional and upsetting for her. She left the room and waited in the hallway as Kat and I continued our investigation.

We began a short session in the room. Kat went into the bathroom where Dawn had felt the strongest negative energy and stood for some time. She felt nothing unusual. In fact, our entire time here was uneventful.

Because Dawn had felt a strong presence in the bathroom, however, before leaving Kat left an audio recorder. What we would discover during audio review the next day was an EVP recorded within a few seconds after we had left the room. It said, "Help me" followed by "here, in here" or "right here."

We continued to investigate the upper floor. If there were spirits here, they remained quiet and unresponsive. After an hour or so it was time to continue our investigation in another location. We headed to the basement.

To us, the basement is the heart of a location. While the upper floors go through renovation and updates, the basement remains relatively unchanged and tells the story of its beginning. The roughly hewn rock foundation at the hotel clearly spoke of its nineteenth century origin. Webs clung to the rafters, their debris-covered tendrils dangled above my head like dozens of frozen raindrops.

Kat, with her bad case of arachnophobia, would not like this. I smiled, a smile of the wicked older sister. Just as I knew, the moment Kat arrived she spotted the webs. Her face twisted in disgust.

"Oh dear God," is all she said. Hmm. I was hoping for more. Oh well.

The basement had a few of these webs.

What immediately caught my attention were the tunnels to the left of the stairway. They snaked under the basement. An occasional bare bulb cast a dismal glow against the rocks and boulders. More webs, in fact a massive amount, covered the low ceiling and walls clear reminders that some kind of unwanted life existed in the caverns.

Scott, who had joined us in the basement, walked over to me as I eyed the eerie tendrils. He mentioned they had investigated in the summer and spiders were everywhere. That did not surprise me.

Taking a deep breath, I moved forward, pulling aside webs as I entered. It was chillingly quiet, like a living tomb. As I made my way to the back of the tunnel, Kat arrived. I turned to see her standing, unmoving, outside the opening. I told her to come in we needed to run an EVP session. Kat tersely replied "Oh hell no!"

My hand batted away one of the dangling cobwebs. "I don't see any spiders." I calmly said. "These are just old webs. They even have dust on them."

Kat's response, "Oh, hell no. I know there are Satan's children in there some where."

Ignoring her reference to spiders (Satan's children), I told her to get inside or she would be walking home from the investigation. Kat muttered unintelligible words, stooped, head hanging low and entered making sure to stay a safe distance from everything.

It was just seconds after she joined me near the back of one tunnel when an EVP was captured. It said, "hurt me." This was clearly not Kat's voice. Another EVP was recorded shortly after our first question was asked, "Is there someone with us in the basement?" The response was a threatening three-word phrase, the middle word a strong curse.

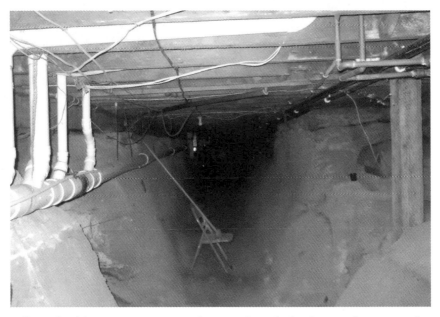

Considerable time was spent in the tunnels with shocking audio captured.

At one point in the tunnels Kat asked, "Can you tell us who's here, your name, your first name?" During audio review the response was "Alphonse," a name that would need to be researched.

Leaving the basement, the most profound statement of the evening came from Kat. She released a deep breath and said, "I have *never* seen so many spider webs in my life." Enough said.

The next stop was the first floor. There was a large suite of rooms where two women and their children were staying. The sweet ladies allowed us time to investigate and went out on the porch taking their young children with them. It was, after all, a beautiful January night with the temperature hovering around 10 degrees. We felt bad about it, but what could we do?

After about a half hour, one of the women knocked on the door and mentioned her three year old was turning blue and her five year old thought her feet were missing. Okay, so the *turning blue* statement sounded serious. We allowed them back in and left. Nothing was captured during the session.

Our last stop would be the much-anticipated antiques shop. This is where Dawn sensed the presence of the man with a pocket watch and a female energy.

It was quiet and uneventful in the antiques shop for the first twenty minutes. Then something caught my eye. "I thought I just saw a shadow… some kind of movement." Since I rarely see anything, this was a bit of a surprise.

Kat asked, "Where did you see it."

I responded, "By Dawn, near the counter."

"I am getting higher EMF readings." Dawn commented, saying they had spiked from a .3 to 1.2. Later, when reviewing audio, we would discover a Class A EVP had been recorded, "Capone."

Capone? Our expectations were to find something linking Frank and Amanda Upright to the hotel. Not in our wildest dreams would we have imagined EVPs that would lead us to Al Capone. The "Alphonse" captured in the tunnels and "Capone" in the antiques shop could only mean one thing, Al Capone. Although we knew Capone had connections and hangouts in Michigan, there was no known link to Al Capone in the Stanton area. It was time to do more research.

Alphonsus (Alphonse) Capone was a first generation American born on January 17, 1899, in New York City. His parents came to America from Naples, Italy. There was nothing special about the family. Both mom and dad were hardworking and proud to be in their new country. Al was always a little different. He was a tough guy from the beginning. At the age of fourteen, he got into a fist fight with a female teacher. When sent to the principle, another fight ensued. Al lost badly and never returned to school.

Al Capone stayed at a cottage not far from here and may have conducted business over dinner at the hotel.

He was often called Scarface or The Big Guy. The nickname *Scarface* came from the three scars on his face and neck he received during a bar brawl in 1917. One year later, after the birth of his son, Alfred, Al married Mary (Mae) Coughlin. That certainly didn't turn him into a respectable family man.

In 1919 he severely beat an Irish gang member in another bar fight. Fearing for his life and family, he fled to Chicago. Al's whole life would change after going to work for Johnny Torrio. Al was just twenty years old but caught the attention of Torrio and soon became his protégé. Al would continue to expand his influence, eventually heading up the entire Mafia organization.

The Mafia made its money primarily from liquor, prostitution, and gambling. During its peak,

Prohibition (1919-1933), Al rapidly rose to power. In order to retain control of the Midwest trade, it was frequently necessary for him to order the elimination of gangs attempting to break in. Also, he would liaison with politicians, judges, and the police.

The bootlegging part of his business brought the Mafia to Michigan in the early 1920s. The Capone Gang ran all liquor sales for Michigan's west side and conceded the East Side to the Purple Gang. Income from his bootlegging was in the millions, and he employed thousands, mostly poor Italians, to deliver the goods. Capone was also notorious for his generosity, continually helping low-income families and communities.

At his core, Capone was a brilliant but ruthless killer. In 1926 his criminal reputation was catching up to him. It was said at one point over 300 detectives were looking for him in Chicago, New York, Canada, and Italy. It became a little too heavy for Capone, and he decided to lay low. His hideout was Lansing, Michigan.

Months passed and Capone knew he couldn't spend the rest of his life hiding. He surrendered to the Chicago police facing charges of murder. It was a wise move by Capone. There wasn't enough evidence to even bring him to trial.

During his time in Lansing, he had a chance to explore Michigan. Capone found some quiet, remote locations that would be perfect to relax away and be safe. Our research was focused on whether or not he had any property in the Montcalm area.

Researching Al Capone's hangouts is virtually impossible. Capone did not want his whereabouts known. He owned no property in his name. In fact, he never made any large purchases of any kind. Property, cars, etc. were always bought in the name of family, friends, or employees. That way he could travel incognito. He didn't want the police, FBI, or rival gangs to know where he was at any given time.

After a very lengthy title/deed search, we were able to find two properties linked to Capone in Montcalm County. Interestingly enough, they were just a few miles from Stanton and the Hotel Montcalm.

Later, a visit with a Crystal, Michigan, historian, Tara Chapko, reinforced the likelihood he spent time in the area. It was believed he had a cottage in Butternut and another at a nearby lake that was registered under the name of a business associate. The historian suspected there was plenty of gang activity in the area, but it was kept very low key, and most residents were unaware or simply refused to talk about it. She mentioned that on occasion Capone would meet and socialize with the Purple Gang, often frequenting their dance club.

One of the best restaurants at the time was the one located at Montcalm Hotel. Travelers or business acquaintances wanting a refined setting and dinner would frequent the lodging's restaurant. Capone definitely liked the better things in life. It seems inevitable he would have gone to the Montcalm for dinner with friends.

Also, it is more than likely a refined establishment like the hotel would have an excellent assortment of liquor in a special room for certain guests during Prohibition. Of course, Capone and his men would be the provider of that liquor. The likelihood of Al Capone and his bootleggers visiting the hotel in Stanton for both business and pleasure is very logical.

Suddenly the EVP "Alphonse" in the tunnels and "Capone" in the antiques shop began to make sense. As we continued to listen to audio, more EVPs were discovered that could be related to a gang connection. This included a very compelling EVP, "Yeah... Chicago... lost the cop." That was shortly followed by, "Yeah, get out of here." The EVPs appeared to be bits and pieces of a conversation.

Two more significant EVPs came from the tunnels. One whispered, "Kill Red Barker," followed by the name "Tommy." Who was Red Barker and was there some connection between Red Barker and Tommy to Capone and the Mob. More research began.

It didn't take long to discover Red Barker was Capone's lieutenant in the Mafia during its heyday. Known as a killer and union breaker, he was a public enemy, ranked just under Capone by the FBI. In charge of unions, it was believed he wanted to succeed Capone as liquor baron. Barker was a real bad one, hungry for power with many enemies in and outside of the organization.

Did we capture gang members planning Red's demise?

Even from his very early years, much of Barker's time was spent in prison, most of it served in Michigan.

On a summer night in 1932, Barker was strolling down the street with three acquaintances. Unknown to them, assassins waited in a hotel across the street. As he passed below, the sudden sound of machine gun fire burst from a window spraying the street where Barker walked. More than a dozen bullets slammed into him, twisting his body backward and down.

Silence followed. Those nearby cowered in doorways, behind cars, or just numbly stood in shock.

Friends rushed him to the hospital, but he could not be saved. Barker was *rubbed out* like he lived his life—violently.

The list of suspects was long and included members of rival gangs. It was Capone's organization that became the primary suspect. Some in the Mafia felt Barker wanted too much power and were opposed to that.

Could the tunnels of the Hotel Montcalm be the location where Capone's Mafia members or another gang plotted the impending demise of Barker? Quiet and remote, the tunnels would be perfect for such a meeting. Suddenly, the EVPs made sense: "Kill Red Barker" and "Tommy."

Was Tommy the man who handled Barker's hit, or was it referencing the weapon used to kill him? In those days, slang for the Thompson submachine gun, the weapon of choice for many Mafia hits, was *tommy* gun. The thought that we may have captured plans to kill Barker was extraordinary.

There was solid evidence for this investigation to support the idea that Capone or other Mafia gangs frequented the Hotel Montcalm. This was an unexpected and remarkable find.

Still, we were a little disappointed that nothing had turned up related to Frank and Amanda Upright. We decided to go back for a second investigation.

Our return would be on a very significant date. Saturday, March 19, was 130 years to the exact day of Amanda Upright's shooting.

That night the moon was unusually brilliant. Its glow cast a cold breath of light that illuminated the empty streets still lined with snow. It had been an unusually harsh winter. For a moment we paused, eyes sweeping the 100-year old storefronts that seemed frozen in time. Even the weather was reminiscent of the day Amanda was shot. Her body left lying in the snow.

Dawn again returned with us. Although she knew the location this time, she did not know the significance of the date. She was very quiet as we entered, I asked why. Her response, "The atmosphere seems very heavy."

"More so than last time?"

"Yes."

Judy, the owner, wasn't there. Instead, her sister warmly greeted us. She told us if we needed anything for the evening to let her know. The hotel was ours for the night, and we immediately ascended to the second level.

We first headed to Room 2. In January Dawn felt this room was used for intimate relationships involving a woman and several men. It was the only room from the first investigation Dawn sensed this sexual tension. Because of that, Kat and I considered the possibility this room was significant to the Frank and Amanda story. We were hoping to gather evidence that would tell us what happened 130 years before.

Dawn immediately felt the presence of a woman. Over and over she repeated the word, "mean." An EVP was recorded then. It was a violent curse. Could the argument between Frank and Amanda have started in this room? Kat and I may have been reading too much into those words. After a few minutes, Dawn shook her head and told us whatever energy had been there was gone.

While contemplating our next move, we stood outside of the room. It was here a second EVP was captured, "Hide her." Those two words seem to add another dimension to our investigation. When Frank left enraged, perhaps a guest or employee at the hotel, concerned for Amanda's safety, asked someone to hide her.

Our investigation of guest rooms continued, saving Room 6 for last. The tension in Dawn's face grew as we neared.

Kat turned to her and asked, "Are you ready for this?" She nodded her head in the affirmative.

We stood in the room for a few minutes quietly watching and listening. Dawn moved toward the bathroom saying she was picking something up from that area. Hesitating a moment, she cautiously entered. Kat was close behind. "What are you feeling?"

"She's hiding there," Dawn said, pointing to a corner of the small room.

Kat stared seeing nothing. "Who is?"

Dawn shook her head; she didn't know who but there was the energy of a woman here. "She is staying right here, and she's afraid to come out."

Entering the darkened bathroom, I focused my attention on the corner Dawn had pointed to and asked, "Why don't you want to come out of the corner? Are you afraid to come out?"

Dawn's eyes narrowed as she picked up the words, "He'll find me."

Dawn still did not have all the details behind Frank and Amanda's story. Yet, what she sensed fell right into place. Was Amanda hiding here from her angry husband, Frank?

We eventually turned to leave. Kat was trailing behind. Before exiting, she paused and made one final plea to whatever spirit may be near.

"We're getting ready to leave. If Frank or Amanda is here, this is your last chance. This is your last chance to tell us what we can do to help you." Several seconds passed in silence then Kat's final words, "This is your last chance."

At that point an urgent whisper was recorded, "Get out now." It was time to escape! Is that what the words meant? A strong residual imprint of the past? Perhaps a former guest or owner at the old hotel telling Amanda that Frank was gone and it was time to make her escape?

It was after midnight when our trio ventured down to the main floor and the antiques shop. Moonlight streamed through the windows casting its silver veil across the room, leaching color from all it touched. There wasn't a sound except for the moan of aged wood resisting our footsteps. Antiques lined the shelves and filled the counters, each one holding the story of its owner. Men, women, and children forever lost to history, these cold objects a lone reminder of their lives.

We stood in silence for several minutes. Dawn paced the floor. What she immediately picked up was the sensation of angry men. They were arguing and threatening each other. She saw the man with the pocket watch again. The same man she had seen on our first visit. This time the man was in the back of the room, afraid to come forward. Kat moved to the area Dawn indicated and took readings. EMF levels were flat and temperatures consistent.

Dawn was apprehensive, "The man with the pocket watch is nervous… threats. There is shouting. Arguing."

Becoming more animated she continued. The argument was over money. Someone was owed money. Having just completed our research on the Mafia and its possible connection to the Montcalm, Kat and I wondered if Dawn was sensing gang members arguing. Were they there to collect money from the man with the pocket watch? Perhaps an owner or shopkeeper at the store owed someone protection money.

Our thoughts quickly changed with her next words. She saw a man storm through the front door with a wooden-handled revolver. The other men were very nervous. The man carrying the gun had a cowboy hat and wore a long coat, often referred to as a range duster worn by cowboys and ranch hands to protect themselves from the elements. Could it be Frank Upright? Was this past robbery Dawn was seeking or was she describing the events that occurred the hotel the day Amanda was shot. Was residual energy re-telling the moments of the event?

As Dawn paced back and forth, another EVP was captured. This one said, "Need the gun."

Finally, putting together all the audio evidence recorded combined with what we knew of the day Frank came after Amanda, a scenario could be pieced together.

On Friday, March 18, 1883, Frank rode into town wearing his long trail duster and hat to protect him from the still frigid air. He went directly to Amanda's room, which we believe to be Room 2, and demanded $25 by the next day.

He had been very upset with her lately because she wasn't making enough money for him. He was also angry about this guy named Charles Chilson. He had heard that Chilson was spending far too much *unpaid* time with Amanda. Chilson was a distraction that kept her from her *paid work*. It could also be Frank was a little jealous. A one-night stand for money was okay but not a serious relationship.

On Saturday, after spending some time at the local saloon, Frank decided to collect his money from Amanda. The terrified young woman pleaded with him asking for just one more day. He became enraged and swore he would kill her and stormed out of the hotel. In fear, Amanda called for help. People at the hotel hid her in another room. We believe it's Room 6.

Meanwhile, Frank went out and bought a revolver. He returned drunk and out of control. The men in the room, now the antiques shop, saw Frank's condition and his gun. They wanted to know where he was headed. He ranted that his wife owed him money and wouldn't pay up. He was going to shoot her. The man with the pocket watch was the frightened shopkeeper. He was nervous, afraid, and cowered in the back. The other men told Frank he wasn't going to kill anyone and asked him to give them his gun. Frank refused, saying he needed the gun, waving it in the air.

The men tried to calm Frank down and told him he couldn't be in the hotel with a gun. If he didn't leave, they'd call the sheriff. Frank left, exiting onto Main Street. He waited as his anger grew.

Thinking Frank had left, Amanda was notified it was safe to leave and fled. The rest is history.

This ends our last investigation at the Hotel Montcalm B&B. Our evidence reveals fascinating stories. Clearly something of its past remains embedded in the walls, rooms and tunnels. We believe Amanda, Frank, even Al Capone and the gang remain. What other spirits reside as yet undiscovered at the Hotel Montcalm Bed and Breakfast? That must be left for a future investigation.

Story Five:
Sam's Joint

(The Red Brick Tavern)
675 10 Street, Plainwell, MI 49080
Phone: 269-586-8235

Password: touched999

Guest Investigators: Dawn James, Kay
VanDrunen, Donald Altman and Lynn Donaldson

THERE HAVE BEEN RUMORS OF the old Red Brick Tavern's haunting for years. Most people in Plainwell know the tales.

We first heard about it during one of our library presentations on the west side of Michigan. Although it's not uncommon for people to share local ghost stories after one of our presentations, this time it was different. Many in the audience told us about one place in particular. The historic Red Brick Tavern now called Sam's Joint.

The basement is reported as one of the most active locations. One former employee, who worked at the restaurant in the 1950s, shared the fact that she was told early on the basement was haunted and no one should ever go down there alone. There have been disembodied voices heard, small fleeting shadows seen, and a general "creeped out" feeling.

Other stories tell of activity more mischievous in nature. They include drink glasses sliding along tabletops and the sound of chairs scraping along floors when no one is there.

Perhaps the most bizarre reports come after hours, when the restaurant is empty. On at least a few occasions, when glancing up at an attic window, people outside reported seeing what looked like a body hanging from the rafters. When checked out, no one was there and the restaurant completely empty.

We've also heard that during one of the restaurant's more recent renovations, a wall was torn down and an old newspaper found. An article was circled. It reported the discovery of small bones on the grounds. The bones were believed to be that of an African American child possibly linked to the Underground Railroad in the early to mid-1800s. We could not locate this particular newspaper article or anything to validate the claim.

Our research took us to Sandy Stramm, a noted Plainwell historian. Her assistance would prove invaluable. She has never heard of this claim. Although an interesting story, the truth remains elusive. With Sandy's help we dug into Plainwell's and the Red Brick Tavern's fascinating history.

Long before Plainwell was settled, it was home to the Ottawa. In the 1830s, the first white settlers arrived. Around the same time, many Native Americans were removed to the territory west of the Mississippi as part of President Andrew Jackson's "Indian Removal Act." Their journey would be a long one.

This was indeed a tragic time for the proud Native American people, but America was changing. As the tribes left white settlements grew and flourished especially around main travel routes.

Plainwell, then known as New Aberdeen or Plainfield, was perfectly positioned at an intersection of plank roads leading to Grand Rapids, Kalamazoo, and Allegan. It quickly became a popular stopping point along the route.

One of Plainwell's earliest settlers was Calvin White. Around 1833 he purchased 160 acres of land and built a log cabin that, in addition to being his home, also served as a trading post and general store.

He built a brick home five years later. It would become known as the Red Brick House and had the unique distinction of being the county's first brick structure.

This distinction is easy to understand when you realize how difficult it was to find brick. Back then the nearest brick kiln was in Marshall, Michigan, roughly 50 miles one way. Oxen would be hitched to a large flatbed board without wheels, called a stone-boat. It would be dragged to and from Marshall.

According to Sandy, Calvin traded 200 pounds of flour for 1,000 bricks. We can only imagine the effort it must have taken to build Allegan County's first brick house. Calvin, no stranger to hard work, must not have minded.

Calvin was a quiet, compassionate, kind man of few words. He was well liked by the town folks and area Native Americans.

In an article written by Sandy Stamm, she shared a story about Calvin that tells us a little more about the kind of man he was. This story dates to the time he brought his new bride home. Upon arriving at the red brick house, all he said was, "I guess we'll have to put up here tonight."

His wife, being very tired from the long, rough journey simply said, "What a pretty place this would be if the yard had flowers instead of corn up to the door."

Plainwell was home to Ottawa tribes long before the white man arrived.

The Red Brick Inn, built by Calvin White

Although Calvin said nothing at the time, when his wife awoke the next morning she saw him digging out the corn with a hoe. She said, "Mr. White, what are you doing that for?"

His reply, "To make a place for your posies."

There were several accounts of Calvin showing compassion for the unfortunate. An example of his compassion was the time when a down-on-his-luck landowner came to him. The man claimed he had no money for food or provisions to hold him over the long winter.

Calvin looked at the man and simply said, "Hmmm." Nothing else. The dejected man left empty handed.

The next day the man heard a wagon approach. He came out of his small cabin to see Calvin's wagon loaded with food and supplies. Surprised and overjoyed, the man said, "I didn't think you were going to help."

Calvin's simple response, "Didn't say I wouldn't."

Over the years Calvin White continued to run his trading post and general store. His red brick inn remained a welcomed resting place for many weary travelers. One of those travelers was James Fenimore Cooper, the renowned nineteenth century author best known for writing "Last of the Mohicans."

James Fenimore Cooper spent the night at The Red Brick
Inn during research of his book, "Oak Openings"

According to records found by a former owner, Cooper stopped at Calvin's place during research for one of his last books, "Oak Openings." It was the summer of 1847. Cooper was traveling along the Kalamazoo River and ended up staying at the Red Brick Inn.

It is especially interesting to note that "Oak Openings" begins with a weary traveler stopping at a trader's home for the night. During the night's stay, they settle down over dinner to discuss politics and the impending war between the Americans and British. Could that have been based on his night spent at Calvin White's home?

By the 1850s main travel routes were lined with boards to improve travel and were called plank roads. They were approximately sixteen feet wide making it easier for wagons to traverse the rough terrain. These early highways played a major role in the development of our state's west side. Once the plank roads came through, Calvin was busier than ever and business was great.

Calvin seemed well suited for the rough life of early settlement days. Sadly, it took a toll on his family. In 1840, within a few months of each other, Calvin lost both his first wife and three-month old son. His second marriage and resulting family suffered equal tragedy. In the 1870s two daughters and his wife died within a short three-year span. After that, this quiet man continued to work his business. It was in 1880 that the toxic poison of gangrene finally ended Calvin's life.

Ownership passed hands many times. Around 1927 Charles Richards took over. He rented the Red Brick House to Carolyn Reed Burton and Elizabeth Reed Pershing in 1928. The two cousins turned the historic building into a restaurant. It has served as such ever since. Sam Bravata is the most recent owner who incorporated it into his expanding restaurant chain called Sam's Joint. That is the name it holds as of this writing.

Our investigation was scheduled for mid-May. Fellow investigator Dawn James would join Bev and me. Also invited were three special guests: Kay VanDrunen, Donald Altman, and Lynn Donaldson. These folks gave us the necessary connections to get approval for the hunt.

We had never been to Sam's Joint and were looking forward to the investigation. Our first impression was surprise. It was difficult to imagine this attractive, well-landscaped restaurant as Calvin White's historic home. Although certainly still brick, it has seen many renovations and expansions over the decades. Perhaps the only telltale sign of its age was the remains of an ancient, nearby tree. Much like the Red Brick Inn, its massive trunk was still standing and still strong.

During dinner our investigative team discussed a strategy for the evening. After a tour by one of the restaurant's managers, Theo, we would break into two teams. In rotations we would cover the basement, first floor, and attic. We had heard the ghost stories; now it was time to see if they were true.

An area of particular interest was the basement where a secret room had been discovered some years back. During one of the many renovations, a section of the old basement wall had been drilled through. Instead of finding a crawl space or opening to the outside, a room was discovered. Its original purpose is unknown. Some believe it may have been a station on the Underground Railroad.

Of course, the Underground Railroad wasn't a railroad at all. Rather, it was a vast network of people who helped runaway African American slaves escape to freedom in the north and Canada. This secret network grew and around 1831 was given the term "Underground Railroad." The term "Stationmasters" referred to those who opened their homes or businesses, called "stations" or "depots" as a place of refuge.

After escaping, slaves would seek out individuals called "conductors" who would help guide them northward to free states. Fugitives usually traveled at night, going ten to twenty miles by foot, wagon, or even boat, to the next "station."

These were incredibly dangerous times for slaves and all those involved in the Underground Railroad. It's difficult to imagine the hardships and dangers they endured for their freedom and this cause.

Was Calvin White a stationmaster and the Red Brick Tavern a station on the railroad? At first we didn't think it likely. Maps showed routes moving well north and south of Allegan County. Certainly none were shown within ten to twenty miles of the Red Brick Tavern.

Sandy Stamm again came through with some information related to the Underground Railroad that might link to the inn. According to a book written by Joe Anderson and John Pahl, "River and Lakes: A History of Allegan County" there was a branch of the railroad that cut through Otsego and Plainwell.

Sandy also shared a story regarding one of Ostego's older homes. It was being torn down when old drawings were found on the walls of a secret room. The drawings seemed to indicate slaves had been there and the room used as a station. This old home was only a few miles from Calvin White's red brick home.

This story is very significant. It could mean the Red Brick Tavern was part of the Underground Railroad. After all, Calvin White was a compassionate man known to help others. He was also a devout Methodist. As historical records tell, Methodists in Michigan were strong abolitionists who wanted freedom for all. Would tonight's investigation provide evidence that would support the story of the Red Brick Tavern as a depot on the railroad?

We wondered if the Underground Railroad activity was the cause for numerous paranormal occurrences in the basement. A fleeting glance of shadows seen from the corner of an eye are one of the reports. Some of the shadows seen were short, about the height of a child. Because of that, it is thought a child's spirit may roam the basement.

As mentioned before, this is the area where people become unsettled. They get a sense of being watched with unseen eyes, a feeling they're being followed when no one's there.

Another area we would target for the night's investigation was the attic. A common occurrence is lights turning on when the restaurant is closed. As previously mentioned, this is the area where reports of a hanging figure had been seen from an outside window. This is also the area where Chris Schultz, Bob Penny and the Michigan Nightstalkers paranormal team had captured the clear, disembodied voice of a little girl.

The main floor would not be forgotten. There were reports of glasses sliding along tabletops, the sound of chairs scraping on the floor when no one was there, and the occasional vision of a fleeting shadow.

The investigation began. Kay, Lynn, and Donald would form one team and head to the attic. Bev, Dawn, and I would form the other team and start on the main level.

Attic where paranormal activity has been reported

The air in the attic was thick with dust, and the atmosphere seemed heavy as the small group entered. They carefully maneuvered around piles of boxes, old tables, and collections of unused items. Settling in one area, they started an EVP session. Questions were met with silence.

Recalling that Michigan Nightstalkers had recorded the voice of a child in the attic they tried another approach. "Do you play upstairs here?"

A sudden, loud bang shattered the silence like a solid ball thrown powerfully against a hard surface. It was followed by the sound of marbles or stones cascading down.

The group stilled, each quickly scanning the room. Nothing seemed out of place. A member of the team cautiously asked, "Are you afraid of us?"

The loud bang repeated and continued again and again and again. Eventually growing fainter until it finally ceased.

Kay, Lynn, and Donald looked questioningly at one another. Nothing in the attic had moved during the entire sequence. They searched in an attempt to identify the sound's cause. For now, it remained unexplained.

During our first break, the excited trio shared their experience. With our very uneventful time on the main floor Bev, Dawn, and I were more than eager to move upstairs to investigate their report.

The first ten minutes were very quiet. EMF levels remained stubbornly flat. We worked our way through the stacks of discarded materials and idly chatted about nothing in particular. Truthfully we were beginning to get a little silly as sometimes happens on quieter investigations. That's when the attic light turned on. We could see it was an old socket and likely old wiring. Paranormal maybe ... electrical most likely.

Not long after that a resounding bang instantly silenced us. It sounded very similar to a billiard ball thrown on a pool table but much louder. The sound was followed by what seemed like a hail of small marbles coming from the roof. It was much like the sound Kay and her group had described.

We immediately started looking for the source. Bev peered out a side window and a portion of the first floor. It was dark, but she thought there was a pile of broken bricks there. Was it a possible reason for the sound?

She exited the building and saw there was additional broken pieces of brick on the ground. She picked up a few pieces and, after several tries, managed to get one to the upper roof. Sure enough, the sound it made was the same.

While outside, Bev decided to check the upper windows where people had reported seeing a hanging body in the window. Standing at a certain angle to the window, Bev did see what appeared to be a body handing from the rafter. It was, however, a matrix. The low incandescent room light created a shadow from boards and boxes that did, in fact, looked like a hanging body.

Returning to the building, Bev met up with Theo. She asked him if he would mind coming up to check the chimney. He was happy to oblige and nimbly jumped up on the roof confirming what we thought. The ancient chimney was crumbling and pieces of brick, in various sizes, lay scattered around. Problem solved.

The remainder of our time in the attic was quiet and a little disappointing. Perhaps the basement of the old restaurant would be different. Unfortunately it wasn't for Kay, Lynn, and Donald who told us their time there was very uneventful. Oh well, some times things happen and some times they don't.

During the break we told the trio about the falling brick. A little disheartened, we all continued with the investigation.

Bev, Dawn, and I headed down to the basement not really expecting much to happen but always open and alert to the possibility.

The first thing we noticed was that EMF levels were high in many areas, ranging from six to over ten points. With normal readings falling under one point, these elevated levels were significant. The EMF bleed seemed to come from the numerous electrical wires and pipes snaking throughout the basement.

Unusually high EMF can affect some people creating confusion, nausea, headaches, delusions, and even paranoia. This could be why so many staff members feel uneasy coming to the area.

In the paranormal field there are many theories, none of which have been proven but are still interesting. One of those theories is that energy can attract or draw spirits. This is a reason some investigators are experimenting with EMF pumps. They're hoping these electromagnetic generation devices will draw spirits. If true, the high EMF levels in the basement of Sam's Joint could be doing just that. We would see what our time here would produce.

Gathering near the opening in the wall where the supposed secret room was revealed, we began a session. The wall separating this room from the main basement was constructed of rocks and boulders of varying size, its exact age unknown.

An opening in the wall revealed a secret room.

The opening was small, and the thickness of the wall all but obscured the other side. In an attempt to see what it looked like, Bev reached in as far as she could with her camera and clicked off a few still shots.

We hoped the photos would reveal some detail that might identify the room's original use. Instead, the pictures showed walls covered with insulating boards, cinderblocks, and little else. It was obvious work had been done during renovations. Unfortunately, it had been cleaned out. Its original purpose would remain a mystery. Also a mystery is where the entrance had been to access this room. It may have been hidden from view.

We placed an audio recorder on the edge of the small opening along with an EMF meter as questions commenced. "Will you tell us your name? " I asked. "Your first name and your last name."

Though unaware at the time, we had already recorded our first EVP. It said a name, "Damien Heathberger."

Inside the secret room.

Our questions continued. Bev stood back, her eyes quickly scanning the room for any movements or sound. She stood near a section of the room where beer kegs were stored. Not long after the EVP was recorded, she glanced to her right. From the corner of her eye a shadow quickly passed. Bev remained silent but became more alert. Then, it came again, quick, sudden, fleeting. It wasn't tall, maybe a few feet in height. That's when she turned to us. "You know I really thought I saw a white shape by those barrels."

Dawn nodded. "I did see a shadow go by me."

Bev continued, "When you guys were talking and even before, a few times I thought I saw a shadow go by."

In an effort to see if we had inadvertently caused the phenomena, we attempted to recreate our positions. This was not easy. After a while we gave up. The shadows could not be recreated. Had it simply been a trick of the eye or was it real?

Dawn started a short EVP session around the barrels. She asked if there was an entity nearby and if they would communicate with us.

"There's no way we can help you unless we know who you are and what you need."

Area where Bev and Dawn saw a fleeting short, white shadow.

Seconds later, an unheard voice was recorded. It didn't initially make sense. After close scrutiny we believe it said, "The bwana" or "mbwana."

We would discover the word "bwana" or "mbwana" is Swahili, a language spoken in many countries in eastern Africa, including Kenya and Tanzania. It is a term of respect meaning mister, sir, master or leader. Was this EVP the response from a fugitive slave suggesting he needed help to escape the "bwana" or his owner? Or was a spirit seeking help from the "stationmaster," the term used to describe the person who gave refuge to those escaping through the Underground Railroad.

It was around this time another EVP was recorded. The voice was different, higher pitched, and sounded like a child. It was one word, "Tayo."

Interestingly, that word Tayo originates from Nigeria. It is a common name given to a male child.

This was a curious series of events. The EVP "Damien Heathberger" was recorded shortly before Bev and Dawn saw the shadows followed by the words, "bwana" and "Tayo." Was Damien Heathberger someone connected to the slave trade or the Underground Railroad? Our search was futile. Who Damien Heathberger was remains elusive.

After a while, we returned to the wall that revealed the secret room and continued our session. Dawn took a small stick and banged it against an old chair asking any entity in the area to respond with a knock. To our surprise, there was a faint rap.

Dawn continued. "OK. If that was you making that noise, I would like you to repeat it. There are a lot of things going on down here. It's very noisy. So for us to hear you I need you to bang on something again. Loudly." With that she again knocked on the chair and lightly, ever so lightly, there was a tap. Was it a response?

Dawn repeated the knock. This time, much louder, a dull thud was heard deep within the basement. We moved toward the sound.

I asked, "Are we coming closer to you?" Can you make that noise again?"

Dawn rapped once more. This time only silence followed.

As we moved further in the basement I felt my left hand begin to tingle, as if a mild electrical current was moving into it. This was very rare for me. I seldom feel anything.

EMF Levels around my hand were within the normal range but very high just above my head. The sensation was likely a result of high EMF.

We continued on, ending in the basement's back room where a collection of old safes was stored. None were original to Sam's Joint. The heavy iron vaults belonged to the owner who collected antiques. Each had been blasted open, the apparent work of bandits.

They were not especially large safes but definitely heavy. The deep black surface of one was blistered with a gaping hole where the lock had been. Another, lighter colored safe, seemed relatively untouched until you moved to the back where dynamite had blown an opening and the edges peeled back to release whatever bounty it had held.

Where they had been, when they'd been broken into, or what was taken remained a mystery. The only thing certain is they were manufactured by the Detroit Safe & Lock Company with the date July 29, 1873 clearly painted on the front. That, unfortunately, was not sufficient information to give us a clue to the past.

Nineteenth century safes, each blown out during robberies.

Another theory in the paranormal community is that spirit energy can attach to objects. We hoped that would be the case with these safes and started another EVP session. Little did I suspect something was about to happen that would later become one of my most profound paranormal experiences.

The session began like most others. We asked a series of questions that seemed to go unanswered. Then, about fifteen minutes into it, I needed to change the tape in my video camera. Slightly distracted, something caught the corner of my eye.

I looked up to see the strangest thing—a quick, flickering light, much like a firefly. I watched as it flittered across the area where Dawn stood. It rapidly blinked on and off with a faint scattering of sparks surrounding it. I had never seen anything like it before. This strange light lasted only a second or two and was gone.

Before I had a chance to say anything, Dawn spoke. "It has to be my eyes playing tricks on me. I swear I saw a little light bounce out of here."

I'd also seen the light, exactly as Dawn reported. EMF levels were checked and, not unexpectedly, were elevated.

Dawn and Kat check out the area where they
spotted a rapidly moving, glittering light

For the next several minutes we tried to identify a possible cause for the strange, flickering light. Our attempts failed.

The EVP session continued. Dawn began, "Is there someone in this corner with us? If it's the same person who was on the other side that we asked to bang on something, can you please..."

Cutting off her words, I quickly pointed to the K2 meter resting on a safe. Up to now it had remained inactive. Suddenly the lights began to flicker.

I asked, "If that's you communicating with us, thank you very much. Can you come closer?"

"I can move away from this if you'd like. Come closer to the gray box," referencing the K2 meter. "Who are you?"

The lights on the K2 flashed once again then quieted. More questions were asked as the second light weakly continued to flicker. It didn't appear to be a direct response and, we decided, likely being affected by the high EMF in the area and not paranormal. Dawn went over, picked up the K2 and repositioned it. The lights immediately went dead.

After some encouragement the K2 again began to react, this time a sudden, stronger response. We could sense the energy building.

Bev and Dawn scanned the room, aware and waiting. I stood with the video camera in my right hand held steady to the area where the safes and K2 meter sat. My left hand was resting by my side.

It was then I felt the touch, a light stroke of three slender fingers on my left hand. They moved slowly downward from my wrist to knuckles. It was a soft, gentle touch. Not aggressive or threatening yet unexpected and a little frightening. This was my first physical contact during an investigation.

A little surprised, I took a quick intake of breath and quietly said, "I've just been touched."

Bev and Dawn turned in surprise. I swung the video camera down to my hand and checked to see if any marks had been left. There were none.

Bev asked if I were kidding. I nervously chuckled and shook my head no just as the video camera went dead. The off button had not been touched. The battery was not dead. It had just shut down.

From that point on, the activity seemed to cease. We were left questioning what, if anything had happened. Later, recorded evidence would reveal something quite startling.

Up to this point we had captured several compelling EVPs that included "bwana" and "Tayo." We also know that Calvin White was a kind man who enjoyed helping others. His Methodist religion told him slavery was wrong. Because of his beliefs and the two recorded EVPs it seems likely the Red Brick Tavern was a station on the Underground Railroad.

The EVP "Damien Heathberger" continues to remain a mystery. We found no one by that name associated with slavery or the Underground Railroad. Who knows, he may have been a passenger on a stagecoach or a former employee of the tavern.

This brings us to my last experience at the Red Brick Tavern. A series of strange events concluded with my hand being touched. During this burst of activity an EVP was captured on Bev's audio recorder.

Bev was reviewing audio a few days after our investigation. I saw her eyes widen as she glanced at me.

"What?" I asked.

She shook her head. "You won't believe this," and handed over the headphones. It was a voice. Old, cracking with age, an unearthly croak that slowly and quietly rasped, "She's the one."

As a paranormal investigator, I am not easily intimidated. There was, however, something in these inhuman words that sent a chill down my spine. Not a threat... more profound.

I'm the one what? Had this entity been searching for me? What did this thing want? To be honest, as much as my paranormal instinct wanted to find out more, my inner self said no.

As my hand lay by my side the fingers that stroked it were slender, like a child's, but lacked the softness. Movement of its fingers downward from my wrist to my knuckles felt as if it had reached up, which would have made it very short. Not much more than two or three feet.

It is believed a child's spirit roams the restaurant. Earlier in the investigation, Bev saw a small, white shadow dart past her. The EVP "Tayo" sounded like a child's voice. However the ancient, cracked words "She's the one" was not the voice of a child but, rather, someone or *something* very old.

Is there more than a child's spirit at the old Red Brick Tavern? Could the small white shadow Bev saw be a child's spirit or another entity roaming the basement?

We went back to history. Before the white settlers came, the land was home to Native American tribes. There is little if any written history as to what happened in those very early years. Before recorded history there was word-of-mouth. Stories passed on through generations. These stories became folklore and legends.

In the years Bev and I have been researching these sorts of things, what we've discovered is that within the fiction there often remains an element of truth, a catalyst that started the stories and created the legend.

We've never relied on folklore to justify paranormal activity. Yet, in this case, perhaps we must. The voice that said, "She's the one," was not that of a child.

Our research continued but this time with a different lean. We delved into ancient folklore and mythology, stories that predate written history. In doing that, something interesting was discovered.

Although each culture has its own mythology, there is one common legend that persists. It is heard in Africa, Europe, China, Great Britain, North and South America. This fable comes from many early civilizations at a time when these cultures were continents apart and unknown to each other. These are the stories about mystical little people.

The Ottawa called them Bgwajini. To the Potawatomis they were Pa'is and to the Africans, Hili or Tokoloshe. Good fiction for late night story telling for sure. Yet, even today many people believe in the existence of these phantom creatures.

According to legend these little beings have existed since the beginning of time. They carry powers that can be used for good, mischief, or evil. Some are said to heal the sick while others can inflict serious illness, even death.

Elusive creatures, they are rarely, if ever, seen. Some legends claim they are spirits, their powers allowing invisibility. Others suggest they exist on different planes or dimensions. Believers claim their movements, when visible, are so quick they are only seen from the corner of an eye as they dart from one hiding place to another.

They hide away from humans preferring the quiet of forests or along rivers and sandy shorelines, such as the Great Lakes. It is also said they prefer enclosed, dark places like caves. With few small, enclosed caves in this part of Michigan, could they have taken refuge within the dark confines of a safe?

Sitting here writing this story, we scratch our heads. Is this even remotely possible? In all honesty, to us it seemed very unlikely, teetering on ridiculous. None of the stories associated with Sam's Joint allude to little people or mystical beings as the cause of its paranormal activity. Yet here we are writing about it. Why?

Do all the strange phenomena reported here have to be ghosts (the spirit energy of a deceased people)? As members of the paranormal community we have to keep a skeptically open mind when something *not normal* occurs. *Not normal* could be many things besides a ghost.

We kept our minds open to this possibility while beginning a second review of audio. This time carefully listening to the entire sequence before and after the touch and recorded EVP hoping there might be something else that would provide clarity.

That's when we heard it, a second voice. An EVP so clear we wondered how we had overlooked it during our first review. Of course, that's the reason we reviewed the audio again. In our earlier excitement over the, "She's the one" EVP, we had missed it.

This newly discovered EVP may hold the answer to that touch and its true meaning. Where this led us presented a completely different possibility. It was something much darker and much more foreboding than the elusive *little people*.

Not long after I had been touched, Dawn asked if we knew where the safes had come from. She was wondering if they might hold some kind of attachment. It was then Bev noticed another EMF elevation. Following that the second unearthly voice was recorded. This time it was higher-pitched yet still best described as a croak. The word it spoke, "Dybbuk."

Dybbuk

The dybbuk (pronounced dih-buk) is Jewish folklore although it is described in Judaism and the Kabbalah in relationship to spirits and possession. The term originated around the sixteenth century and, in Hebrew, means *clinging spirit.* It is considered a malicious or malevolent spirit, the soul of a dead sinner seeking to possess or *haunt* the living.

It is not a demonic possession. Rather, it is the soul of a once living person who does not or cannot move on to the afterlife because they are a sinner.

They continue to wander the earth for several possible reasons. Fear is the first. They fear the punishment awaiting them in the afterlife for their evil deeds on earth. Another is that God has blocked them from entering the afterlife because of their terrible sins. Yet another reason is unfinished business.

The dybbuk seeks refuge and is capable of *haunting* earth-bound things whether it is a blade of grass, a living being, or even a box. Of course, a dybbuk's preference is a human. They look for someone who has committed a secret sin or has made themselves emotionally vulnerable. This will open the door for the dybbuk to enter the body of the living and attach itself.

The only way to release a dybbuk from your soul is through exorcism or death of the living host. Once the dybbuk is released, it will seek another refuge, whether it is another living being or the confines of something quiet, secure. There it will wait, patiently, until it is released to seek its next victim

A dybbuk box has been spoken of in movies, television, and written in books. It is said to be a wooden Jewish wine cabinet haunted by a dybbuk. As long as the cabinet remains sealed, the dybbuk is contained within. Once it is opened, however, the malicious soul is released. Can a dybbuk only haunt a wooden wine cabinet? Could it *haunt* or attach itself to a safe?

Bev and I sat back at the conclusion of this story, this investigation, and contemplated all that was recorded and researched. There is paranormal activity at the old Red Brick Tavern. Although there may be activity occurring in the attic and main floor, during our investigation nothing noteworthy was recorded in those locations. For us, the basement held the key to activity. The African words, "bwana" and "Tayo," lead us to believe this place was connected to the Underground Railroad. The name, Damien Heathberger remains elusive, although one day we hope to discover who he might be.

Then, of course, there are those antique safes in the back room of the basement. We know little about where they had been or what happened at the time they were broken into. We know even less about the individual or individuals who owned them or the robbers who blasted them open. How deep were their sins?

It is certainly possible someone may have been killed during the robbery. If so, had their sins in life been so profound they remain on earth fearful of afterlife retribution or were they blocked from entry by the hand of God? Have their malevolent souls remained attached to these large iron boxes, patiently waiting for the next vulnerable victim. Was I their chosen?

As I sit alone this early April evening, dark storm clouds approach and I wonder, have I changed?

Story Six:
Eaton County Courthouse

Courthouse Square Association
100 West Lawrence
Charlotte, MI 48813
517-543-6999

Investigative Team:
Mid Michigan Paranormal Investigators

Password: cha8511

Iₜ ᴡᴀꜱ ᴇᴀʀʟʏ Jᴜɴᴇ. Nᴏᴛ quite summer but the temperatures still hovered in the low nineties as we headed out to join our paranormal pals, Matt and Melanie Moyer from Mid Michigan Paranormal Investigators. The night's investigation would take us to Charlotte, Michigan, and the 1885 Eaton County Courthouse.

Back in its day, the courthouse was the heart of Eaton County government and, until 1976, a powerful symbol for the community. Some of state's most noteworthy trials were held here. Within its walls the final word of law was spoken, verdicts decided, and lives changed forever. Justice, and sometimes injustice, prevailed.

It is currently preserved as a historic site, managed and maintained by the Courthouse Square Association. Though government and court offices have been relocated, there are still operating offices on the first floor. The employees who come to the old halls of justice on a daily basis were the ones that contacted the Mid Michigan team for help.

Although unexplained phenomena had been going on for years, in recent months the activity had increased. It reached a point where some employees refused to work after dark or be the first to enter in the morning.

The unmistakable sound of chairs scraping along floors in vacant rooms, hushed whispers of disembodied voices, objects moving across tabletops, and fleeting apparitions were putting staff on edge. They hoped a thorough investigation of the building would give them some answers.

Adding to the night's work would be an investigation of the former Sheriff's residence. Built around 1873, it now served as home to the Chamber of Commerce. Although no one reported strange activity at the sheriff's old residence, the group decided to include it in the night's hunt.

Bev and I arrived in Charlotte as the sun began to shift lower in the sky. Streets literally shimmered casting off their stored heat in the cooling temperatures of approaching night. The buildings in this quaint, historic district were well preserved, transporting us to another time. The old buildings combined with the hazy shimmer of heat cast the town in an eerie, almost dreamlike time warp.

Downtown section of Charlotte

Turning our car onto West Lawrence Street, the Eaton County Courthouse and adjacent Sheriff's residence came into view. The classic Renaissance Revival architecture silenced our idle chatter. It was nothing less than imposing. The courthouse's massive construction and towering bell tower clearly represented what it was meant to be, the gateway to unquestionable authority.

The nearby sheriff's residence was equally compelling. Bev smiled and glanced at me, "I don't know if the sheriff's residence is haunted. If it's not, it should be. Look at that thing! Disney could not do better."

In truth, it did have the classic haunted house look. The architecture was Victorian Italianate with flat roofs, molded window caps, ornate, curved eaves ending with a turreted tower at the very top. Its brick exterior was painted medium dark red. If someone called it blood red, they would not be wrong. Indeed, it was a pretty darn good stereotype of a haunted house. Of course, long ago we discovered that looks are very deceiving. Whether or not spirits actually existed within the old home, we hoped to find out tonight.

Courthouse designed in Classic Renaissance Revival style

Sheriff's former residence

Members of the Courthouse Square Association, Mid-Michigan
Paranormal Investigators with authors, Kat Tedsen and Bev Rydel

Matt, Melanie, and team had already arrived. We joined them
and were quickly introduced to Julie Kimmer, office manager for
the Courthouse Square Association, and Sue Rodriguez, a legal
secretary who had worked in the old courthouse for several years.
Sue had personally experienced some of the unexplained activity
and would be joining the group for the night's investigation.

After introductions, Julie and Sue escorted us into the
building. The interior was incredibly cool and refreshing after the
extreme outside heat. I mentioned to Julie how wonderful the air-
conditioning felt. She laughed. There was no air conditioning. The
thick walls and massive construction simply kept the first floor
cool. With a wicked grin she added, "That'll change as we get to
the upper floors."

She was right. The cool air quickly vanished as we made our way upward.

The second level introduced us to the courthouse proper. It held a series of rooms once serving as county offices and the Probate Court. Rich, honey-colored wood edged walls and covered staircases. Our gaze lifted upward through the levels of floors that circled an open atrium. High above, at the very peak, was a beautiful stained glass ceiling. Yes, it was definitely impressive. How truly grand it must have been in 1885.

Our group followed Judy down the hall. Our footsteps and voices echoed off the walls surrounding us in a reverberating cacophony of sound.

It was immediately apparent the open design of the building created a grand echo chamber. That would present a real challenge for audio recording later that night. The slightest whisper or sound of a team member might easily create a suspect EVP. Adding to the challenge, if a spectral voice or unexpected sound did occur it might be hard to trace its origin.

Judy took us into each room, now filled with a collection of antiques and other historical artifacts. In one chamber, Bev and I spotted an old sign tacked on a wall, "Charlotte Sanitarium." The name was familiar as was its proprietor, Dr. Wallace E. Newark.

Charlotte Sanitarium

At the turn of the twentieth century, Dr. Newark was a well-respected physician of the community. In 1900, based on the rapid expansion of patients in the area, he opened the Charlotte Sanitarium, sometimes referred to as Newark's Sanitarium.

It was in 1903 when the good doctor's career was placed on hold and the reputation of the sanitarium and its physicians questioned. It would be one of Eaton County's most controversial trials. A trial involving a crime so unthinkable, so sinful in this early post-Victorian time it would only be spoken of in whispers or late at night when children were fast asleep.

It was near the end of January 1903. A young man, W. H. Wirtz from Marshall, Michigan, came to Charlotte seeking treatment at Dr. Newark's sanitarium for Harriet, his young bride of just two weeks.

Dr. Wallace E. Newark

Dr. Newark, after speaking to the couple at length, agreed to take on Harriet's case and suggested they move to the Bush boarding house in town for further treatment. Apparently, at some point, a surgical procedure was performed by Dr. Newark. After that, Harriet's condition grew worse. Other surgeries followed and with each her condition deteriorated.

Harriet's husband, deeply concerned over his wife's declining health, called in another doctor who, upon assessment, told the couple he would only take the case if Harriet signed a sworn statement before an Eaton County judge that detailed Dr. Newark's actions and released him of liability. Sadly, the day after Harriet signed the statement, she died. Based on the statement, Sheriff Oliver Halladay arrested Dr. Newark on a charge of murder.

Rumors quickly started. Eventually the reason for the arrest came forward. Harriet was pregnant. It was believed Dr. Newark had attempted to abort the pregnancy. His inept surgery led to her eventual death.

It was sensational, to say the least. Not only was the reputation of Dr. Newark placed in question but also the ethical practices of the Charlotte Sanitarium. Controversy continued for the next several months with growing concerns that abortions and other questionable medical practices were being performed.

Dr. Newark's well-paid attorneys provided skilled defense. After a hung jury and much negotiation, the charge was reduced to manslaughter. Newark eventually pled guilty to a lesser charge, was fined a nominal fee and released. Without valid evidence to further the claim of abortions or malpractice by either Dr. Newark or the sanitarium, the outrage quieted and eventually disappeared. Dr. Newark continued his role as proprietor of the sanitarium until his death in the 1920s.

Back to the present, we turned and followed Julie who directed us to the area that once served as the Probate Court of Eaton County. It no longer resembled a courtroom. The judge's bench was gone as were other semblances of courtroom appearance. It was now filled with a variety of antiques and period memorabilia.

From there, Julie led us upstairs to a set of heavy wooden doors and stopped. Turning she pointed to the wooden rail surrounding the upper floor.

"In the early 1970s there was a gentleman who was ordered to pay a great deal of back child support. After the hearing, he ran out of the courtroom and jumped over the railing to the floor below. He didn't die but did break both of his legs." It seems he paid one way or the other.

Interior of Circuit Court

Julie turned back to the large doors and swung them open to reveal the circuit court. It remained in a beautifully preserved state. A tall carved wood arch highlighted the front wall and beneath it the presiding judge's bench. To the side was a small platform and chair for the witness. Beyond that was a raised platform with twelve chairs that served as the jurors box.

Fleeting apparitions and disembodied voices had been reported here and throughout the corridors of this floor. It would be an area of focus for the investigation.

Julie continued to lead us upward. With each succeeding level, the air became more stagnant and the heat oppressive. Because there were only vague reports of suspect activity on the top floor and with the intense heat more than a little overwhelming, the Moyers decided to focus the night's investigation on the second and third levels where the majority of activity was reported.

With our tour of the courthouse finished, Julie took us to the sheriff's residence. Most of the first floor had been converted to Chamber of Commerce offices. The original living room was now filled with computers and modern office equipment. A small kitchen to the back remained relatively intact with a side room being used as storage.

From there we headed to the second floor. This level contained a series of rooms once serving as bedrooms. In later years, the rooms became apartments. Today, they were used mostly for storage. One of the larger rooms was set up with a table and served as a conference room.

Before ascending to the top floor, Julie briefly paused. She explained the original jail house had, at one time, sat directly behind the sheriff's home. A number of years back it was torn down when it became structurally unsafe and the cost of repair too high. The open yard behind the sheriff's quarters is the area where the jail once stood.

Early Sheriff's Residence shows the jailhouse extending from the back

Julie continued to explain that, while the main jailhouse was gone, part of it did remain. It was located on the upper floor of the sheriff's residence where women, children, and those considered insane were held.

It may sound strange that prisoners, some considered very dangerous and criminally insane, would be kept so close to the sheriff's family. This practice, however, was not uncommon. Their close proximity allowed the sheriff to keep a constant eye on them and be on hand instantly if a problem arose.

Julie cautioned our group to watch our steps as she led us up the narrow, rickety stairway. We entered through a worn, fractured door and instantly met with an intense claustrophobic heat. It felt very much like stepping into a sauna wrapped in a heavy, wet wool blanket. The air was old, stale and some unknown, unpleasant odor lingered, immediately putting me on edge. I stepped over a broken floorboard and heard something crunch beneath my feet. Looking down I noticed the floor was covered with small dark pellets.

"What's all this?" I asked as my foot nudged the pellets aside.

Julie shrugged, "Oh, I guess there are a few bats that live up here."

In unison our group looked upward, eyes scanning the rafters in search of the creepy nocturnal creatures. None were seen. Hopefully it would stay that way during the investigation. With a quick grimace I gingerly stepped away from the *pellets*. Lovely.

We slowly explored the uppermost floor. Prison cells were gone with not a single reminder of their earlier existence. A fire had gutted the area many years before, and the charred reminder of it could still be seen in the scarred rafters and skeletons of broken walls.

Perhaps it was a combination of oppressive heat; dark, ravaged surroundings; and pungent odor but the atmosphere was different. As much as none of us wanted to spend time here, we knew this would have to be another target area for tonight's investigation.

The faint, orange glow of the setting sun cast hazy shadows across the aged floor and walls, signaling the approaching night. It was time to go.

Matt and Melanie Moyer organizing equipment for their team to set up.

As we exited, faint stirrings could be heard above us. Bats were beginning their night vigil. I glanced back one last time to see dark, inky shadows shifting in the upper rafters.

Back in the courthouse, the team quickly set up equipment. Night vision and full spectrum video were positioned in the courthouse. Hand held equipment would be used for areas the DVR system could not reach.

The investigation began. Bev joined Melanie's team in the courthouse while I went with Matt's team to the sheriff's quarters.

A faint breeze helped cool the hot air as our team headed to the home. I looked up into its levels of dark windows half expecting to see a ghostly face peer out. Nothing.

Begrudgingly, I admitted the old Victorian home seemed more than a little eerie in the darkness of night. But then night's dark veil always does that. It makes wherever you are creepier. With limited vision, our minds almost always contemplate the possibility of something unearthly, unseen lurking just out of sight.

We entered the foyer and main hall of the sheriff's house. Matt and teammate Tony began taking EMF readings. Levels were unusually high, most likely generated by computers and other office equipment. With such high EMF fluctuations, it was decided to abandon use of EMF gauges for this floor.

Slowly we moved from room to room. During one EVP session in the kitchen, Matt and Tony thought they'd heard a voice coming from the basement and went down to investigate.

I stayed on the main floor to quietly observe. What must this room have looked like without all the modern office furniture and equipment? Based on the size, it seemed likely at least two original rooms had been merged to form this larger area now used as office space. Most likely it was a formal dining room and parlor or living room. Certainly this was where the sheriff and his family spent most of their time.

Many sheriffs had served Eaton County over the past century. The one that immediately came to mind was Oliver A. Halladay.

Halladay took office in 1902 successfully serving two terms. Sheriff Halladay was politically smart, maintaining strong ties with town leaders. He was considered ethical and highly moral, but his term was not without controversy.

Downtown Charlotte at turn of the century

Halladay was an advocate for justice, but in 1903 those traditional values would be challenged. What if legal justice failed? Should vigilante justice prevail? What is the truer justice when a great injustice has been done?

The turn of the century was a volatile time in Charlotte, Michigan. People were just stepping out of strict Victorian beliefs. A new freedom was beginning but not yet accepted. It was a time when women had few rights and depended entirely on a man for their care. It was a time when an unmarried, working class woman struggled to survive. Should an unmarried woman become pregnant, she was in an impossible dilemma and her future nearly hopeless.

The Phenix House and Charlotte Williams Hotel

It was the morning of November 2, 1903. A housekeeper at the Hotel Phenix in Charlotte was going about her normal cleaning duties when she discovered the lifeless body of a young woman hanging from the transom of her room. The maid knew who the dead woman was. In fact, most in town knew her name. It was Mabel Sturdevant. She was a pretty young lady who worked as a part time waitress and domestic. Mabel had come to Charlotte a few weeks earlier, after a failed suicide attempt in Eaton Rapids.

What caused this young woman's hopelessness? Her apparent love for a rather unremarkable desk clerk working at Charlotte's Williams Hotel: J. Ward Copeland.

Copeland was not particularly good looking nor was he tall, standing well under 5'6". At the time, he was somewhere in his forties with thinning, light brown hair and a large moustache that nearly consumed his small face.

Copeland was considered mentally challenged. When seventeen, he severely injured his head in an accident. At the time, it was thought the head injury had killed him. Copeland was to be buried. It was during the funeral he "came back" to life.

Perhaps it was the trauma of his head injury or the horror of waking up in a coffin at his own wake that changed Copeland forever. After that, he as never right in the head. It was written he had the mental capacity of a fifteen year old.

In spite of this and his overall unremarkable appearance, Copeland was said to be a ladies' man. He knew the right words to say and easily gained their favor. Married and divorced at least once, he constantly had his eyes on new women friends. Young, innocent Mabel had been one of them.

Although Mabel knew Copeland for several years, it was after Copeland's divorce, during a June expo in Buffalo, New York, where their friendship developed into something more. Copeland charmed her and she fell madly in love.

Over the summer she came to visit him several times, eventually moving to the area. Copeland quickly grew uninterested and sought the affection of other ladies. He told her to leave. She refused, professing her love, but he no longer cared and simply wanted her out of his life.

Eventually, not wanting to deal with the situation, he left town without a word to anyone, including Mabel. Mabel was prostrate with grief. Reports said she was unable to leave her bed.

Prominent town leaders of Charlotte took an interest in the young woman. She explained that Copeland had professed his love, vowed marriage, and then had abandoned her. To support her claims she turned over letters Copeland had written that confirmed her words.

The men in Charlotte sympathized with the innocent young woman and their anger at Copeland grew. No one knew where he had gone. Even his boss and good friend, George Williams, knew nothing of Copeland's whereabouts. It was not long after that Mabel took her life.

An autopsy revealed Mabel Sturdevant was pregnant. The father was believed to be Copeland, a result of his seduction in New York. The death of Mabel was placed fully on Copeland's shoulders and town leaders rallied for justice.

They called for the Prosecuting Attorney to file a warrant for the arrest of Copeland citing abandonment. Anger grew higher when the Prosecuting Attorney indicated there was not sufficient evidence to issue a warrant.

That's when the town leaders decided to take action. If the law would not serve justice, they would. In their minds, Copeland had wronged the girl in a most profound way. They would be ready for him when he returned.

Unsuspecting, Copeland did eventually return. When the owner of his rooming house refused to let him in, Copeland sought a friend who provided details. The friend left Copeland with a warning not to go into town unless he wanted trouble.

With little money and nowhere else to go, Copeland disregarded his friend's advice and returned to Charlotte and the Williams Hotel. He knew his friend, George Williams, would let him stay there until he could figure things out. It turned out he would not have much time to "figure things out." The town leaders soon discovered he had returned and was staying at the Williams Hotel.

Prominent people of the community immediately began organizing their vigilante group. Hundreds of men flooded the Main Street of Charlotte.

Fearing for his safety, Copeland phoned the sheriff's office asking for Sheriff Oliver Halladay's protection. Neither Sheriff Halladay nor anyone from his office came.

It was around 8:00 p.m. when the mob charged the Williams Hotel. Copeland, hearing the angry shouts and seeing the approaching masses, rushed upstairs to his room locking himself in. Within moments they broke open the door, found him hiding under the bed, and dragged him out.

As soon as Copeland appeared outside, the crowd's angry rumbles turned to cheers. He was thrown to the ground in front of the hotel and was swarmed. Struggling was useless as the angry crowd tore the clothing from his body.

Now, naked and helpless, he awaited his fate. A small group of men pushed their way through carrying a vat of some black, inky substance. In an instant Copeland knew what it was, tar.

He tried desperately to get away but was held firmly in place. They covered him with the sticky, thick, hot liquid then assaulted him with clouds of feathers.

The taunting quieted as the leader came forward and told Copeland he had 24 hours to leave town. If he returned, he would get the same treatment but next time much worse.

Copeland, humiliated and in fear, cowered on the street as the satiated crowd left. He quietly raged with anger that they would do such a thing to him. He knew who the mob's leaders were and he would make them pay for this.

The next day, emotions were at a fever pitch. The previous night's event didn't calm the town but seemed to ignite a growing, volatile unrest. An excited crowd erected a rather grotesque effigy of Copeland in front of the Carnegie library. A sign was hung with the words, "Remains of J. Ward Copeland."

The Carnegie Library where angry townsmen
rallied to seek revenge on Copeland

Threats were moving beyond Copeland to George William, proprietor of the Williams Hotel. He was being called an accomplice and equal in fault.

Sheriff Halladay finally stepped in knowing things were really getting out of hand. He quickly deputized a number of trusted citizens and strategically positioned them along the streets to keep the peace.

Copeland took the first train out of town while George Williams and his lady friend quietly vanished. With all culpable parties gone, the rage slowly dissipated.

It would, however, not be the last Halladay or the town of Charlotte heard from Copeland. Within a few weeks, he sought out attorneys in Lansing and multiple lawsuits were filed. The first was against Sheriff Oliver Halladay on allegations of his failure to respond to his request for protection. Next, assault and battery charges were filed against each of the prominent members of the town who led the vigilante group.

The sheriff, after being served, claimed that he had been sick that day and by the time he summoned his deputy, the deed had been done and the crowd disbursed. The underlying belief, however, was that Halladay had deliberately not taken action because he quietly sided with the mob's vigilante justice. And, of course, considering prominent members of the community led the action, it was politically smart the sheriff not get involved.

It wasn't long after the lawsuits were issued that the Prosecuting Attorney made a startling revelation. He had just gained sufficient new evidence to warrant Copeland's arrest for "being wholly responsible for the death of Miss Mabel Sturdevant."

Copeland backed away. All lawsuits were dismissed. Within a year Copeland returned to Charlotte and resumed his position as clerk at the Williams Hotel. However, he was never free from the memory of his humiliation or blame from Mabel Sturdevant's suicide.

The years that followed took a toll on Copeland. Rheumatism crippled him. The degenerative disease resulted in amputation of a foot. Copeland died in 1918, without a penny to his name, a cripple in the county poorhouse.

Over the decades, the memory of that early November night in 1903 has been forgotten. History, however, continues to tell the story.

My mind came back to the present when I heard Matt and Tony return from their investigation of the basement. I asked if the basement area was more interesting.

Matt shook his head. "No, not really. It was very quiet although EMF levels are really high." It's not uncommon for EMF levels to be unusually high in a basement. Electric circuit boards and wiring from the house are usually down there.

Leaving recorders running on the first floor, we headed to the second. EMF levels in this area were relatively flat. We settled in the conference room where Matt began the EVP session.

"If there's anyone here that would like to communicate, we're not here to hurt you in any way. If you can hear us, we're trying to talk to you."

After a pause, he continued, I'm going to tap twice and I want you to tap twice too."

With that Matt lightly tapped on the table. We waited in silence. Our attention was drawn to the K2 meter sitting on the table between us. Its lights flickered briefly. Additional questions followed without further response.

At one point, Matt repositioned the EMF meters a little farther away from us. Then the K2 began to give up periodic responses. Not all associated with questions. That led us to believe the elevations were coming from a natural source in the room. Surprising, it was discovered an old, unused steam radiator was the culprit. Certain metals naturally generate high EMF. In this case, it was the radiator.

Matt shrugged, "Well, it's good we found the cause. Are we ready to go up to the top floor?"

Carefully, we made our way up the narrow, broken stairway entering the top floor. It was void of most outside light, its darkness requiring a few moments for our eyes to adjust.

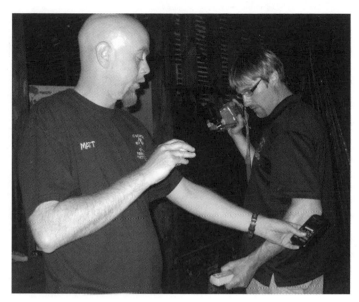

Matt and team member, Tony, check EMF levels
in the Sheriff's House upper floor

Matt and Tony started their EMF check. As they did their rounds, I entered the larger room to the left. Standing completely still, I quietly observed. Nothing remarkable.

I snapped off a few shots with my digital still camera. The camera flash sent powerful bursts of light into the room. I stopped to check the pictures. The first couple of shots revealed nothing of interest, but I paused over the third. There was a dark blur on the lens, a streak of black. The next picture showed the same thing, this time a bit larger. It was the fifth picture that was revealing. Oh no.

At that moment, a rush of air swept within inches of my face. Involuntarily, I raised my hands over my head as I quickly stepped back. Damn bats!

That was my first introduction to Peppermint. At least that's what I decided to call her. The name was so completely inappropriate it seemed appropriate.

Peppermint was not just any kind of bat but a large female. She was dark, brownish-gray body with a white under belly. She swung around the room and headed right towards me.

Introduction of Peppermint the bat

She knew where I stood, of course. Though a bat may not see well, their fine-tuned sensing sonar called echolocation allow them to know exactly where everything is even in total darkness.

This time I stood my ground. She shifted not more than a yard or two in front of me moving so swiftly I barely noticed her dark shadow slide past. It was immediately followed by a second and a third. Oh great. Just fine. Peppermint's entire family was here.

I edged my way out of the room toward the hallway just as Matt and Tony were entering. Should I tell them? Before I could make up my mind, Matt shot several still pictures. His flash, like mine, flooded the dark room with a powerful burst, and I knew I didn't have to say anything. They were quickly introduced to Peppermint and her friends.

"Damn!" Matt ducked as two bats shot past him. "There are a bunch of them up here!"

The two men soon joined me in the hallway. We decided to keep our still cameras in their cases. No more flashes! After a few minutes, the frenzy quieted. We cautiously continued our investigation of the upper level.

Another EVP session was about to begin. Matt had his K2 and the more precise Mel-Meter with him. I thought we might place another K2 further away and asked Tony if he had one. He did not. I fumbled around in my bag for a few seconds and couldn't find it.

I searched the room and found it sitting behind some debris on the table behind me. "Must have put it back there when I first entered the room." We were set and our next EVP session began.

The upper floor of the Sheriff's residence once served as holding cells for female and children prisoners and those deemed insane

As Julie had mentioned during our tour, this dreary area had once held women, children, and prisoners deemed *insane*. How awful it must have been up here with little light and stagnant air. Freezing in the winter and steaming hot in the summer.

Sarah Love was one of the prisoners kept here. Imprisoned after her stepson had made claim she was dangerously insane. But was she? This was another controversial case in Charlotte that clouded Oliver Halladay's term as Eaton County Sheriff.

Sarah Love was an interesting woman, a woman ahead of her time in many ways. Before she met and married Harrison "Tip"

Love, she had been Sarah Watson, a private, independent woman, who owned her own farm. This was a remarkable and almost unheard of thing in the 1800s. In some areas of the country, women were not even permitted to own land.

Women were also not supposed to have an opinion or, at least, not voice it. They were expected to be virtuous, reserved, care for their children, and obey their husband.

Sarah was not that kind of woman. Because of her independent, private nature, many considered her strange. She was also a mystery. Townspeople knew little about her. They weren't even sure if she had a prior marriage before Tip Love or even if she had children. They only new she lived alone on the farm and came to town infrequently.

Sarah married Tip Love at the age of forty. The marriage occurred just a few years after Tip's first wife had passed. Tip's nearly-grown son, Burton, joined his father on Sarah's farm. Burton was not fond of Sarah and *tolerated* her until he moved away a few years later. After moving away, he was rarely seen by Tip or Sarah.

Sarah and Tip's marriage continued for twenty years, and it seemed a good enough fit. Sarah and Tip appeared content. Sadly, in 1902 Tip passed away from heart disease and Sarah, at sixty years of age, was once again alone. Although Tip was gone, she still had her house and her land. That was enough.

Unfortunately, Burton and his family who had come for the burial decided to move in. They didn't ask Sarah if she wanted them to stay or even ask if they could move in. They just did. Burton and his family were never a part her life, and Sarah immediately suspected their motives. They wanted her farm.

The truth was, Burton thought the land was his by right. Although the land was still in Sarah's name, after the marriage Burton believed the farm became his father's and now belonged to him.

Sarah was beside herself. The land was hers! Perhaps for the first time in her life, she felt completely powerless. Over the next year there were many arguments. The battles escalated. Burton and Mary threatened to put Sarah in an insane asylum if she kept acting up.

It was too much. One cold February evening in 1903, Sarah and Mary had an usually heated argument. According to Mary, Sarah attacked her with a pair of shears. Mary immediately went to Burton. Without hesitation, he put his wife and child in a wagon and headed into town and Sheriff Halladay's office. It was already 9:00 p.m. and getting late when the couple arrived at his home. They insisted Sarah had become violently insane and they feared for their lives.

The sheriff did not believe it was as serious as Burton claimed. Neither Halladay or his deputies were eager to leave their warm homes at such a late hour. So the sheriff, knowing that Burton was motivated by money, offered to pay him to care for his stepmother until the next day.

Burton would have none of that. He told the sheriff if anything bad happened to any member of his family because the sheriff hadn't taken action he would hold Halladay and his department personally responsible. Halladay contacted the probate judge and, based on his recommendations, relented and personally went out to the Love farm, arrested Sarah, and brought her to the woman's prison.

Sarah was enraged and humiliated. She was not crazy! Didn't the sheriff understand or care that her stepson was trying to take her land?

When Sarah arrived at the prison, two physicians were brought in for an initial evaluation. They couldn't make a determination as to her sanity at that time and decided to wait a few days for a second evaluation. In the meantime, Sarah sat in a dark room above the sheriff's residence.

Finally, Sarah's personal physician came into the mix. He adamantly attested to the fact he'd known her for years and she was completely sane. He further added his belief that the charge was trumped up by her stepson in order to take her land.

A second evaluation by physicians confirmed that Sarah was "normal" and the claim of insanity branded as fake. Momentarily vindicated, Sarah headed home only to discover her stepson had taken over the farm and locked her out of the house.

Sarah did not give up but decided to fight back. She hired attorneys and filed a lawsuit against her stepson for false claim. It was soon after that Burton and his family packed up and left. Sarah joyously returned to her farm.

She filed a second lawsuit again Sheriff Halladay in the amount of $10,000 for false imprisonment. A trial was held. The evidence was clear and the jury found Halladay guilty.

Sarah's jubilation was short lived when the amount of damage claim given was not $10,000 or anywhere near it. It was just $5.00. The jury stated that, although Sarah had been falsely imprisoned, the sheriff was only doing what he thought best.

Again anger and frustration flooded her mind. It was a slap in the face and Sarah believed just another great injustice done to her. There was nothing more she could do but return home. There she remained in relative solitude for the next eleven years.

It was early November of 1914 when the fire struck. Her beloved farmhouse was burning. Neighbors came to help, attempting to extinguish the flames, but it was too much. The house was burning and Sarah refused to leave. A few brave men ran into the flames and literally dragged her out just as the walls began to collapse.

When it was over, the home and all of her possessions were gone. Sarah had nothing left. She lost her home that day and with it a piece of her heart and mind. With little money, she was unable to rebuild.

Although for years some thought reclusive Sarah was crazy, perhaps now they were right. In 1917 Sarah Love was deemed insane and committed to Kalamazoo State Hospital. She remained there until her death in December 1919 dying from pneumonia at the age of seventy-six.

There is no doubt one of Sarah's most traumatic moments was her time locked up on the third floor. Frustration, sadness, and incredible anger over the injustice must certainly have charged her emotions. I wondered if any of the energy from that trauma remained locked on this floor.

I spoke Sarah's name, "Sarah Love, are you in here?" Empty silence followed.

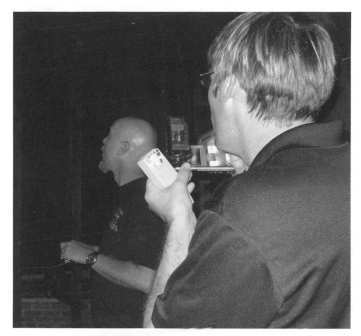

Matt leads an EVP session with team member Tony assisting

Matt began, "Hello, Sarah. We know you weren't crazy. We know you're not insane. We know you were held here against your will. Sarah, are you here?"

Over the next thirty minutes we continued our quiet vigil. Once or twice the K2 meter's lights flickered, but nothing seemed in direct, consistent response to questions. As far as our group was concerned, only the bats resided here. We would, however, discover during audio review we may have been mistaken. Two rather compelling audio pieces had been captured.

After I had asked the question, "Sarah Love, are you here?" A high pitched voice, obviously female, responded with a quick, "Yes." The recorded voice was so clear I was surprised I hadn't heard it.

At the time Matt said, "We know you were held here against your will," a response was recorded, "They won't let me go." Sarah, perhaps, pleading to us that the sheriff wouldn't release her from the dark prison cell.

Another EVP was recorded at the time I was looking for the K2. I had found it sitting on a table behind me. Moments before that, a voice clearly said, "Look behind you." It sounded very much like a child or woman. Was one of the former women or child prisoners trying to tell me where the K2 sat?

Our time in the sheriff's residence was over. We headed outside to meet up with Melanie's team at the designated time, but they were not there. We waited and waited. No one appeared. Then Melanie's voice came through on the walkie-talkie. Something had happened in the circuit courtroom and they were investigating.

The team eventually came out to join us in the front yard. "So what's up?" Matt asked.

Melanie explained, "I think we may have gotten something in the circuit courtroom. Bev and Sue were sitting on the benches and head a voice out in the hallway. There was no one in the entire courthouse but us, and we weren't talking at the time."

I looked at Bev, "Really?"

Bev firmly nodded, "Definitely."

Bev and Sue heard a voice just outside the courtroom doors.
Audio review would confirm the disembodied voice.

In all of our many investigations, Bev very rarely has had a personal experience. Her definitive response was surprising.

"We were in the first row of the courtroom," she explained. "There were no questions being asked at that exact time. I heard a woman's voice. It was a fairly high-pitched voice. It was two syllables." Neither Sue or Bev understood what the words were, but Sue thought there it sounded like "hi" or at least a strong "I" sound. Both were certain it was a female voice.

Wendi Fournier, another member of the team, had also experienced some strange things in the circuit court. It was a black mass, about three-quarters up on the wall. She reported seeing it twice about five minutes apart. The darkness was not in the form of a person but rather, a very shapeless form that blocked the light momentarily. Wendi was unable to find an explanation.

Another member of the team, Rich Childs, added that it was around that time minor EMF fluctuations registered. A scratching noise was heard, like feet scuffing along the floor. Following that sound was a bang. Wendi shook her head. It was the craziest thing, the activity just seemed to kick up then was gone.

Unfortunately, video did not capture the black mass and the shuffling sound was not captured on audio. However, the voice Bev and Sue heard was on audio. A very clear, female voice said, "Step aside."

Could this have been a residual energy? Perhaps the voice of someone wanting to leave a busy courtroom asking those blocking the doorway to step aside?

Matt, eager to see what his team might encounter, headed our group straight to the circuit courtroom. Melanie, not particularly interested in meeting Peppermint in the Sheriff's residence returned to the circuit court as did Sue.

We positioned ourselves around the courtroom. Melanie sat at the judge's bench while I sat at a table on the side where the defense team would have been. Matt positioned himself at the prosecution's table on the opposite side.

For some time our group sat quietly and just observed. My eyes drifted around in the colorless gray of the darkened room. The circuit court's ceiling far above gave this entire area a sense of vastness.

I suggested it might be a good idea to conduct a mock trial, thinking it might stir up some activity. Matt agreed. Unfortunately, our efforts went unanswered and the entire building remained frustratingly quiet.

Matt and Tony wait for Melanie to take the judge's
bench for the mock trial to begin.

Eventually, I turned my focus on the judge's bench. Some of Michigan's most horrific criminals were convicted and sentenced here. Certainly during the conservative Victorian Era, the most infamous murder trial was the Canfield Wretch, Dimondale Murder. The hearing associated with the conviction hadn't lasted long. In fact, it was just one day but remains one of the most sensational.

It all started with the horrible discovery of a young girl's naked body in the Grand River near Dimondale in late January of 1891. The poor little girl was found wedged under a log in the chilled waters. She had been brutalized and strangled. The community was absolutely horrified. Eaton County Sheriff Pollock was immediately called in.

The deceased child was not more than ten or eleven. The young girl was Nellie Griffin, an abandoned child living at the Coldwater state school for the poor.

Newspapers described Nellie as a smart, beautiful girl with short cropped dark hair and large, stunningly blue eyes. Though she was pretty, her life had not been. In fact, her life was nearly as tragic as her death.

Nellie was the product of passion and definitely an unwanted birth. Her mother abandoned the family shortly after she was born, and her father was apathetic and uncaring. By the time Nellie was three her father took the child to his parents to raise and left town.

For the next several years, little Nellie remained at her grandparent's farm. Her grandfather, the former mayor of Mason, was a tough disciplinarian and described as a "gruff, uncouth" man. He and his wife considered the girl a burden and cared little for her.

By the age of eight, Nellie began to take every opportunity to escape her loveless home. She would often disappear late at night and would be discovered hiding on dark stairways or other out-of-the-way places.

Neighbors complained and Nellie's grandfather would have no more of her. He signed a complaint for her "wayward" ways. During the hearing it was determined she should be sent to reform school. A few compassionate townspeople stepped in saying the sentence was too harsh for the young girl who had done nothing to hurt anyone.

Her grandparents would not take her back. So in December of 1888, she was turned over to the superintendent of the poor and sent to the state school in Coldwater.

The Coldwater state school was a place where abandoned, abused, and orphaned children were kept. It was overcrowded. Beds filled small rooms and lined the hallways. Children spent long hours in classes, studying, or working. There was little time for play. Some children were indentured to farms or manufacturing plants. Indentured work was a form of slavery where the poor would put in long, grueling hours without pay.

A lucky few at the state school would find themselves adopted to good, loving families. But, even with adoptions, little was done to make sure the children went to loving households. Many ended up in a worse situation than the harsh, loveless conditions of the state school.

Nellie, according to school reports, was an excellent student and her behavior exemplary. It was on a fateful day in late January 1891 that a man in his fifties came to the state school. The name he stated was false, but he would later be identified as Russell Canfield.

Canfield told the superintendent he was looking for a ten or eleven year old girl. People who knew Canfield would have told the superintendent to be wary. The man was a strange sort who admitted to having an unusual enjoyment of young girls.

The superintendent, of course, knew nothing of Canfield or his character. The superintendent may have brought out any number of girls at the school fitting that description. As it turned out, it was Nellie the superintendent first spotted and brought to meet Canfield.

"Will she do?" The superintendant asked. Canfield looked her over and told him yes. Arrangements were made for Nellie to be transported by train to where the man lived, which was in Dimondale.

The train ride would be the last time anyone would see little Nellie alive. It was days later her body was found.

Canfield was arrested and taken to the Eaton County Jail. Newspapers reported that when he was shown the ravaged body of the girl he showed no emotion, only swore his innocence. He claimed to have never seen her.

However, the state superintendent swore with absolute certainty Canfield was the man who had come to the school asking for a girl. Others at the train depot also confirmed he was the one who had taken Nellie.

Finally, after a lengthy interrogation by Sheriff Pollock, Canfield broke down and confessed. He had killed the girl. It was an accident.

He admitted going to the state school and picking up the girl at the train depot. He also admitted heading on foot toward his home. Somewhere along their walk home Canfield decided to deviate from the road. He could not tell the sheriff why he had done that, saying only that he did. He led Nelllie down a remote path to a quiet section of the Grand River.

According to Canfield's statements, he didn't remember exactly what happened next. They were sitting on a log when the girl started to cry. He attempted to calm her down without success. He confessed to placing his right arm around her shoulders, his left hand over her mouth. Next thing he knew she was dead.

Canfield continued saying he removed her clothes before throwing her in the river because he thought the clothing would prevent her from sinking. He swore her death was an accident and further swore that he had not molested her.

The truth was revealed when Sheriff Pollock finally uncovered the girl's clothing from under the floorboards where Canfield lived. They were shredded, the sleeves completely ripped off. Holes torn in her undergarments and a considerable amount of blood.

The autopsy report confirmed what the sheriff and others believed. Young Nellie had been assaulted then strangled to death. Adding to the evidence against Canfield were gray hairs, similar to his, found on the girl's clothing.

The people of Charlotte, enraged at his barbarous act, gathered in town. They sought vigilante justice, and this time nothing but a lynching would suffice.

Sheriff Pollock, knowing he would be unable to hold off the mob, did not waste time arranging for a court hearing. Canfield quickly admitted guilt before the circuit court judge who followed his guilty plea with a sentence of life at Jackson Prison. Within hours of the sentence, he was taken to Jackson Prison. There he spent the rest of his life.

As for little Nellie, her tormented, loveless life was over. Nellie's remains were given to the nearby Presbyterian church where she was quietly buried in their small cemetery. There she remains, finally at peace.

There are so many stories connected with this circuit court. So many powerful, life changing events, we wondered if any residual energy was left?

I pulled a folded paper from my pocket. Weeks prior to our investigation, Bev and I had collected several names of Eaton County judges and sheriffs along with the names of those had been tried and sentenced in this courtroom. I began calling out names on the list and information related to the arrest and trial without apparent response.

At one point Matt asked, "Canfield, are you here?" He paused and repeated in a firmer more demanding voice, "Mr. Canfield, are you here?"

There was a quiet tap. Tony asked if we heard it. We had heard, but it was so faint it could have simply been the building settling. I followed up Matt's question.

"Mr. Canfield, are you here?"

Then came the sound. Quiet, rushed, almost urgent. Matt eyes scanned the room then looked at me, "What was that?"

I'd heard it too, a voice, a single word. It certainly had not come from one of us and there was no one else in the entire building. We would later discover an abrupt, "No" had been recorded. Unfortunately, that elusive voice was not heard again and offered no explanation as to who it was or why it remained.

Just before the end of our scheduled time in the courtroom, we conducted another short mock trial—no defendant in particular, just a series of typical statements one might hear. I acted as defense team attorney and Matt prosecution.

At the end, Melanie asked the jury for their verdict. Then, after a brief silence, Melanie loudly spoke, "The jury says guilty." Then she asked me, "Do you want to poll the jury."

"Yes, your Honor, I do."

At that point Melanie began the poll, asking each unseen juror to confirm their verdict. The sounds in the hallway began just around the time Melanie asked for juror number three's response. Faint but audible footsteps were heard several times in the outer hall. There was no one there.

Melanie slowly, calmly continued polling the ghostly jury, the faint footsteps still shuffling in the outer hall.

She asked for juror number seven's response and, sensing that some event was about to happen, in the same calm breath directed us, "Somebody go stand in that door and watch."

Before anyone had a chance to move, Matt's voice cut in, "Right there!" Pointing toward the open courtroom door. "Did you see it?"

He'd seen a shadow, in the shape of a person, rapidly moving past the doorway. "Did you see it, Melanie?" Matt asked.

"No. Go look." Her voice remained controlled as her jury poll continued. Matt, Tony, and I swiftly moved to the hall. There was nothing. When Melanie was done with the jury poll, she and the remaining members of the team gathered in the outer hall.

According to Matt, the shadow suddenly stepped into view from the left side of the hall, peeked in the courtroom, momentarily blocking the light, then just as quickly retreated into the darkness. We could tell from Matt's excitement that he clearly believed what he had seen.

Unfortunately, nothing was captured on video or audio to support Matt's vision. Another frustrating moment and one that is all too common on investigations.

Without recorded proof of what was seen or heard, it's just another story and not evidence. This holds true no matter how certain an investigator may be. It's just too easy for human error. A brief, reflected light from a passing car headlight or a bounce from a laser light or even IR light can be misinterpreted.

Although Matt couldn't validate what he'd seen, he was convinced it was real, very real. This evening's investigation was ended, but the hunt wasn't over. We would be coming back again. Next time, the team would be ready should the shadow make a second appearance.

So it was that several weeks later we once again found ourselves back at the old Eaton County Courthouse. Knowing the layout and the areas to focus on for this night's investigation, the team got right to it. Within a short time video was positioned focusing on the circuit court and the group was broken into teams.

Matt, Melanie, and the team wanted to focus on the circuit court while Bev and I preferred to focus on the sheriff's quarters.

Leaving an audio recorder on the main floor, Bev and I moved upstairs to the second. Ascending the staircase I called out, "I'm looking for the sheriff. Is he here? Sheriff? We've returned, Sheriff. We need to speak with you."

Without audible response, we entered the second level and positioned ourselves in the conference room just as the lonely ring of the bell tower sounded. Bev and I settled down to the session.

With no unusual sounds or K2 hits, it was time to move upward and say hello to Peppermint and, perhaps, the ghosts of the top floor.

As we pushed through the ancient door to the old prison room, the intensity and unease that hit us during our first investigation was still there. This feeling wasn't a result of the flying night rats or the area's ravaged disrepair. It was just something that permeated the atmosphere, wrapped itself around you, and wouldn't let go.

Within seconds of our arrival on the top floor, an eerie male voice was captured on audio. Its tone demanding, "What do you want?" The last word "want" spoken in a hiss and drawn out.

Moments after the first EVP, a second was recorded. Another voice, the words began with a graphic swear word followed by "... get them out!"

Our investigation of the upper floor continued as did our questions. We left an hour later, happy that Peppermint and her family had stayed restful.

Since Matt and Melanie's team were still in the courthouse, Bev and I walked over to the yard where the old prison once stood.

It was a few minutes after 1:00 a.m. Streets were deserted with only the occasional rumble of a passing car.

It is believed spirit energy remains not just within a structure but may also attach to the ground. With that in mind, Bev and I settled in and began a session in the yard.

Of course, Russell Canfield had been imprisoned in the old jailhouse so his was the first name I called out. "Russell Canfield, you admitted killing Nellie Griffin."

We were later surprised to discover an EVP was recorded immediately after this statement. The responding words repeated his name, "Russell Canfield."

We continued asking a series of questions, but all remained quiet. In fact, the air around us was even unusually still, only the day's heat and humidity seemed to linger with us in the yard. The unnatural silence remained for some time.

It was during this time, two very clear EVPs were captured. One said "Venku" and the other a much quieter "Zocor." After extensive research, we were unable to find those names associated with the courthouse, prison, or even past town residents. During its time, the jail not only held those awaiting trial but also wandering vagrants and homeless people. Most of their names are lost to time.

After thirty minutes or so, Matt and Melanie's team emerged and joined us outside. The activity on their investigation was much quieter and review would later indicate no evidence recorded.

Since that day, we have not returned to the old courthouse or sheriff's residence. There are so many stories that remain unknown. Countless souls are embedded in the very foundations. Perhaps, even now, they continue to wander the halls and rooms seeking answers, justice, or just release from their eternal confinement. For now, their stories remain untold.

Story Seven:
Clive and Dot's Anchor Inn

1781 Heightsview Dr
Houghton Lake, MI 48629
(989) 202-4153

Guest Investigator: Dawn James

Password: khg1755

SITTING BACK AND RELAXING ON a hot summer afternoon, we were reviewing our rather hectic fall schedule. That's when the all too familiar ping on my computer sounded. An email had just come through. It was a message from a woman named Ronda Spears and sounded paranormally urgent. We followed it up with a phone call.

Ronda and her husband Jason manage Clive and Dots Anchor Inn, a local bar/restaurant, in the popular vacation community of Houghton Lake. Recently, paranormal activity was picking up in this 100-year-old building. She wasn't sure why unless all the recent renovations were stirring up the spirits. From what Ronda told us, the Anchor Inn had a long reputation of being haunted, going back long before she managed it.

Earlier in the year, her parents, Clive and Dot Clymer, purchased the inn and major restoration was underway. According to Ronda, her family and customers were having experiences. The activity occurred almost daily and included doors opening then slamming shut, objects moving, footsteps, disembodied voices, and apparitions.

The stories about Anchor Inn fell into the haunted category. For this hunt we would be bringing fellow investigator and good friend Dawn James. Dawn believes she has a certain amount of sensitivity, often able to pick up people and events from the past. She is always welcome to join us.

Driving into town, we passed the shoreline of Houghton Lake. The town hadn't changed much from what we remembered and brought back some fond memories, like fishing on the lake with our dad.

I recall being horrified the first time we went fishing. Every time a fish was caught, we would plead for its life. Dad looked at us and, shaking his head, returned it safely to the water. On future fishing trips, he changed our bait to peanut butter and jelly. We never did catch another fish, but we had some great times fishing on the lake with Dad.

Turning off the main strip, this part of Houghton Lake was unfamiliar to us. In the dusk of early evening, the white shingled bar stood out. Dawn, Kat, and I surveyed the area. It was a quiet part of town, even for November, but a few cars were lined up in front of the inn. Leaving the car, there was a chill in the air signaling winter was not far behind. As we approached the inn, warm yellow light and laughter streamed from the windows.

We stepped through the doors and stepped back in time. It was similar to the restaurants our family would go to many years ago, simple and friendly. From behind the bar, Ronda waved and came to greet us. How did she know who we were? When we asked her, she laughed and chuckled and said, "You're the only ones I don't know." After introductions she took us on a tour.

As our group moved upstairs to begin, an all too real looking torso of Freddy Krueger and his infamous slashing fingers startled us. Ronda chuckled and told us to just ignore the scary decorations. Halloween was the week before, and they hadn't taken down the props from the haunted house attraction Anchor Inn operates in October.

Moving beyond the glaring eyes of Freddie, only a few lights illuminated the second floor. Their hazy glow cast long, faint shadows across the hall. Rooms to the right and left appeared as small, dark caves holding secrets of the inn's past. The main hall seemed to stretch on forever and ended at an enclosed porch that contained the second light on the floor. Debris, tarps, and ladders reminded us of the ongoing renovations. The inn's age showed in its worn, creaking floors and broken ceilings.

We slowly walked along the dark hallway. Dawn stopped between the first and second room on the right. "I feel like someone was being held captive... forced to stay unwillingly... it was kept hush-hush." There was more than one person. She was quiet for a moment, serious, her eyes darting. Dawn was getting multiple spirits and a lot of activity. She needed to move away from the area, the sensations were too strong and too sad.

Moving farther down the hall, Dawn stopped before another room and entered. There was a single bed against the wall. Its mattress was old and cracked with dirt. She shook her head. There had been sexual activity here and she backed away.

Dining area reminiscent of a 1950 restaurant

Freddy Krueger was a scary figure that gave us nightmares

Dawn experienced a number of emotions on the second floor

In the room closest to the porch, Dawn felt someone happy, dancing. She also picked up on several men that appeared to be from the 1920s, 1930s, or 1940s. Who they were or why they were there she could not say.

She continued her walk through on the opposite side of the hall. Our small group followed. Stepping into a center room, Dawn stopped. There was sadness here, a woman crying, filled with grief—the kind of sadness felt when someone you dearly love dies. Dawn couldn't determine who died or when it happened.

Dawn finally ended her walk-through in the room just to the left of the entrance. Her hands clenched momentarily as she sensed an angry young man.

Ronda, silent until that time, nodded her head in acknowledgement. This had been the office. She thought Dawn might be picking up the spirit of Danny, the son of a former owner. Involved in running the business, he spent a good deal of time in the upstairs office helping his father. One of the greatest tragedies in his family was Danny's sudden, tragic death. It happened when Danny was living downstate. Although he didn't die at the restaurant, Ronda believes his close ties to the place may keep his spirit here.

With Dawn's walk-through over, Ronda began sharing the eerie tales that persist about the bar. It wasn't until renovations began they would learn the stories were true.

One of her recent encounters was at the entrance to the second floor, where she saw a woman standing. When Ronda described this woman to the former owner, he immediately knew who she was talking about. Marie Best was an interesting and colorful past owner of the business.

That brings us to the to the history of Houghton Lake and the Anchor Inn. Ronda, a history buff, filled us in on much of the past.

The community began in 1883 as a lumbering settlement known as the Heights. Lumber proved lucrative for many years. It started to change after the turn of the century when land around the lake was developed. Businesses grew that catered to sportsmen and vacationers. The Heights became a very popular destination from the 1920s through the 1950s. It still remains one of Michigan's most popular tourist and fishing spots.

Back in the day, the waterfront was known for its nightlife. Old timers fondly recall the dance pavilion, Ra-Walla Dance Hall. Located by the beach, it was a very popular summer hangout. Crowds would gather at the pavilion, listen to the sounds of big bands, and dance till the wee hours of the morning.

Rumor has it that the 1920s and 1930s brought in the Purple Gang and Mafia during Prohibition. The bars along the lake needed to provide refreshments to their guests. Bootlegging, gambling, and adult entertainment proved very profitable for the mobs.

Over the decades, highways and freeways have changed the downtown area of the community. The Anchor Inn, once in the middle of all the activity is now in a quieter section of town.

The inn was built about 100 years ago, and was called the Akin Hotel after the two brothers who built it. They successfully ran the operation until the 1930s. Over the years it had several owners before the Clymers purchased it.

In the 1960s it was sold to Ira Best. Upon his death the hotel/lounge was turned over to his wife. That brings us back to Marie Best, the apparition Ronda was telling us about.

This historic hotel was called Cliff's in the 1940s.

Marie was one of the bar's more colorful owners, managing it until the 1980s. She ran the hotel and restaurant adding one more dimension, a beauty salon on the second floor. Ronda found a diploma from the La-Mar Beauty Academy made out to Marie Isabel Yon, her maiden name. Interestingly, if you flip the diploma over, on the back is a cut out portion of a "For Sale" sign. Was the diploma fact or fake?

Ronda shared that, according to the town's old timers, there was more than a beauty salon on the second floor. They claim Marie was the madam of a rather high-class bordello. There are no records to confirm this, but Ronda tells us longtime residents swear to it.

She also heard that in the late 1960s or early 1970s a murder took place here. It was a stabbing that was extensively covered in the local newspapers. Our research got us nowhere. Although we could not verify the claims of a bordello or the murder, Ronda seems certain it was true.

Marie Best may be one of several spirits that remain at the Anchor Inn. Comparing her description of the apparition she saw with some old photographs of Marie Best, she may be right. Marie's spirit could remain because of her deep connection to the town, hotel, and possibly the murder. But then, do we really know why spirits sometimes stay where they stay?

Marie Best with two friends.

This is the point where Ronda mentioned the suicides. There were several associated with former employees. Suicide is not common. We wondered if the inn was somehow associated with these tragedies. If so why?

With that said, she shared another bizarre experience. Ronda and her daughters were working when they all saw an open ladder slide across the floor. None of them were near the ladder when it happened.

Even Jason, Ronda's husband and a skeptic, has had many experiences. He refuses to go up to the second floor alone, day or night.

Their daughters, Kaitlin and Miranda, have had other strange occurrences on both the first and second floors. Kaitlin mentioned hearing her name called while she and her boyfriend were on the first floor, a little unnerving since no one else was around. Kaitlin also experienced doors slamming for no reason.

Marie, Danny, and the other spirits may not be the only entities that remain here. The family fears there might be something darker, more sinister and perhaps inhuman.

Miranda recounted her most frightening experience that occurred just a few weeks before our visit. She was with her cousin at the time. They were walking towards the back room on the second floor. It was around dusk. She gasped, thinking she saw a shadow figure. They checked but found nothing.

It was dismissed until strange noises were heard. The two young ladies peered into the dimly lit hallway. To their horror, a silent, black figure stood. The intimidating mass was wide and about six feet tall. Its legs disappeared into a heavy mist rising from the floor. Afraid to leave, Miranda urgently texted her dad to come get them.

As they waited, their eyes were frozen on the hallway, afraid of what might come next. Miranda wondered what was keeping her father. Then it happened. Another dark mass darted passed them. Much lower to the ground than the first, it looked like an inhuman creature or animal maybe three or four feet tall. They each held their breath, waiting for something to happen. It did not.

Thankfully, her father arrived and brought them downstairs. He was there in minutes, but to the frightened girls, it seemed like hours.

This would not be the last time Miranda experienced something out of the ordinary. One day Ronda and other family members were upstairs. When Miranda didn't respond to a question, Ronda turned to her daughter. Something wasn't right. Miranda was acting strange, unusually quiet, and unresponsive.

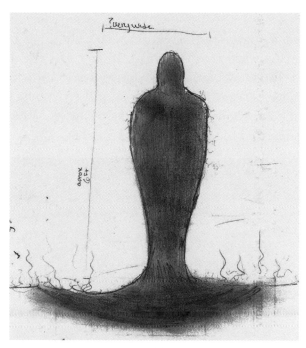

Dark shadow seen on the second floor, sketched by Miranda.

Second shadow seen, sketched by Miranda.

Once downstairs, Miranda told the group she had felt odd and claimed to have seen something dark standing by her side. At the time she wasn't scared or sad. In fact, she felt no emotion whatsoever. There was an overwhelming sense of being trapped, unable to move. It was difficult to explain. As Miranda was telling the story, she mentioned her back was burning. When checked, they were surprised to see three large scratches.

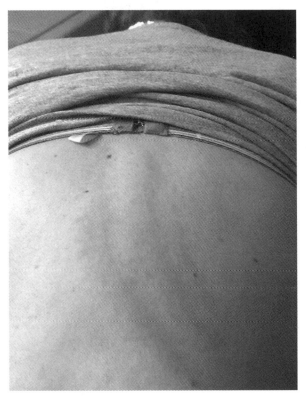

Miranda's scratches

Many members of Ronda's family and circle of friends have experienced strange phenomena on both floors. Could they all be wrong? Ghost stories are like a yawn, very contagious. In the dark when someone has a frightening experience, the likelihood of others believing the same thing is happening to them is possible. So was the Anchor Inn a case of paranormal hysteria or was there something unexplainable really going on?

As with all of our investigations, the stories were compelling, but we needed evidence. Tonight's investigation may give us some answers.

After the tour and interviews, we went downstairs to plan the evening's strategy. It was then Dot Clymer, Ronda's mother and owner of the restaurant/lounge, arrived. Dot shared her own personal experiences that included voices and shadow people. She also recounted some of her guests' stories. There was no doubt in her mind the place was haunted and likely had been for many years.

L to R: Ronda and Dot talk about their experiences.

Since so many occurrences seemed to happen on the second floor, that's where we would start. As night descended, a noticeable chill filled the long hallway and empty rooms. Halloween props added to the creepiness.

For the first part of the investigation Dot and Ronda joined us. If the spirits were familiar with these ladies, they may respond more readily. Many paranormal teams believe spirits become more active once they know you. That's one reason why some will investigate a location multiple times.

We reached the second floor. Kat was still by the entrance, near Freddie, while the rest of us continued walking towards the back of the hall. We heard her call out, "Ya know, I thought I just heard someone say sssh. That's what I thought I heard." I didn't hear anything and neither did the others. Later we would learn that an EVP had been captured, "Shit." It clearly did not come from us. Was it residual or a spirit upset to see our group returning?

Kat thought she heard a voice

Moments later, audio recorders were positioned around the floor as our EVP session began. Kat turned on her video recorder and we were good to go.

Everyone positioned themselves along the hall. In the half-light we found chairs to reduce the creaking from the warn floors. My first questions: "Was this a booming place when you were here, Marie?" I continued asking questions directed at Marie when another voice, soft and raspy, "Get out." was captured on audio. None of us suspected anything.

First the word "Shit" then a minute or two later "Get out." If the spirits didn't want us there, we wouldn't know till several days later when reviewing audio.

A chill was seeping into our bones as Kat began talking to Danny, "Don't be afraid of anything. We're certainly not here to harm you.... Danny do you know you're dead? A direct response followed. One simple, clear, word, "Yes." Was this proof that Danny's spirit remains at the inn?

About mid-way through the investigation, Kat started questioning, "Was anyone hurt here?"

A clear raspy voice would be discovered later, "Yes, suffer." The inn saw a lot of activity from the mobs and Marie Best. Some may not have been pleasant

It seemed like our group attempted to draw out the spirits forever, but nothing happened that we were aware of. Even Dot and Ronda tried cajoling the entities. There was absolutely no reaction or feeling by any of us. When we first reached the second floor, the spirits seemed to respond, but then it all faded. Kat thought that maybe they didn't like our energy.

Whatever the reason, we decided to move downstairs and see if our attempts would be more warmly received. Dawn, Kat, and I vowed to return to the second floor later in the evening.

Around 12:30 am the session on the first floor started. We were hoping to pick up on the apparitions seen, disembodied voices, and doors slamming that people have experienced.

We all gathered around a central table in the dining room.

At about 1:15 am, Dawn heard a voice coming from the hallway. She thought it was a woman saying "here." She took Kat to check it out but found nothing. That's when they decided to investigate the men's room, also rumored to be active.

There just a few minutes, they suddenly heard a loud bang, almost a crunching—like wood breaking. It seemed to vibrate the floor around them. A heart stopping moment. Involuntarily, Dawn grabbed Kat's arm. What was that? They began to search for the cause and found a floorboard that was similar, but not nearly as loud. Could that have been the source?

When they came out, we decided to move to the bar. Kat thought she heard a noise coming from the hallway again. She went to check and, even though she heard nothing, the audio recorder captured an EVP. The voice was soft but strange because each syllable seemed to be carefully enunciated, "Why don't you get here?" Those words reminded us that earlier Dawn thought she heard the word "here." Was this the same voice and did the spirit need our help?

Then things settled down. Minutes seemed like hours. Ronda broke the silence by telling us about all the paranormal activity in Houghton Lake. She claims, "It's very hard to find someone in Houghton Lake where you don't talk to them and find out there is something going on." Traveling across Michigan, Kat and I have heard that before. On occasion people will tell us their whole town is haunted. We have always found this to be a curious statement.

In spite of being exhausted, we decided to go back to the top floor one last time. It was nearly 2:00 am, and the floor seemed more charged than before. It's hard to explain unless you have been on an investigation and had that feeling. It's an internal sense of anticipation.

Although we were ready for anything, the night was very quiet. While sitting idle we decided to review some of our earlier video and photos. That's when the shadow was spotted on our video camera. It looked very much like the one Miranda had described, tall and wide, shaped like a mummy in a casket

Looking at each other in surprise, it quickly faded as we realized it was Ronda.

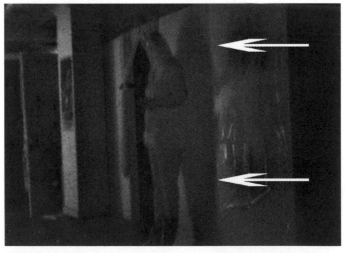

Shadow from Kat's video similar to the one Miranda saw

The shadow moved as she moved. Did Miranda and her cousin, in their fear, mistake one of their shadows as the terrifying image in the hall? This often happens. However, the four-legged shadow creature was another story. We could not recreate anything that even remotely resembled that figure.

Getting back to the investigation, we decided to place a hat on the floor. Earlier Ronda told us about the ladder she and her daughters saw moving. Well if poltergeist activity happens up here, we were hoping to catch it.

Kat said, "Could you move the hat on the floor?" Although the hat didn't move, an EVP was captured. A raspy voice said, "They are weird." Perhaps the spirit thought our request was odd.

This EVP seems to suggest someone or something was watching us. According to Ronda, many folks get that feeling at the restaurant. Maybe they are right. Personally, I felt nothing and neither did Kat or Dawn.

About 3:30 am we wrapped up and headed out. Just what evidence was collected would not be discovered until a few days later.

Back to the office we went, put on the headphones and started listening. It was the craziest thing. We recorded numerous EVPs during that evening. This kind of event rarely happens to us. In only a handful of our investigations, perhaps three or four, were this many voices recorded. Many were too quiet to be understood; yet the murmurs could clearly be heard.

The possibility of outside sound contamination was dismissed. Our investigation took place on a Sunday night in early November. The street was completely deserted.

Some voices seemed to respond to questions or things we were doing. Others were just random words, likely residual. Most could not be connected to the history of the Anchor Inn. It's almost as if we were in a subway or train station listening to people passing by.

The inn has seen a lot of history in its 100 years. We weren't able to find documents or records to prove any of the stories and hearsay. Whether it was a gang hangout, bordello, or site of a notorious murder continues to remain a mystery to us. Yet, these stories remain fact for the town folk who believe them.

For us it was frustrating. Then we stopped and thought perhaps, for this investigation, history was not the key. Perhaps more important was how so many EVPs could be attached to one location and recorded in such a relatively short time?

We turned our focus to a few different areas. Just a couple of days before our investigation there was major solar flare. The next day it was followed by another major flare. Scientists warned they were so strong the energy burst could affect audio transmissions. Could these high-energy bursts affecting the earth be attracting or pulling spirits. This may be the reason for the numerous EVPs.

Continuing to approach the investigation differently, we also turned to a relatively new field of research. It involves the earth's magnetic energy and spiritual powers. This research is referring to ley lines. The concept itself is not new and goes back thousands of years, but researchers are looking at its possibilities with renewed interest. Does this reveal an ancient knowledge that has been lost over time? It is a complicated theory. We're not experts. Far from it. Yet, the basic premise is fascinating.

In the 1920s, it was thought ley lines were simply travel paths between two points.

Anyone can connect two dots with a straight line. There is nothing unique or spiritual about that. However, what researchers discovered were these geographical straight lines connected a series of ancient structures, locations, or mystical sites.

Is this just a coincidence, or was something more powerful at work? Many ancient sites and significant points around the world occur along these lines. Current theory implies ley lines can and sometimes do span the globe. Ancient monoliths—structures or monuments—were set up along ley lines to control energy that connects through the earth's grid. Stonehenge is connected to a major ley line.

Many believe that spirits, memories, and actions flow along ley lines. According to theory, when two ley lines cross they form a portal, a flow of energy into or out of the earth.

To our surprise, two major ley lines intersect right in the Houghton Lake area. We discovered the website of Peter

Champoux, www.geometryofplace.com. He is a noted theorist on ley lines today and his book Gaia poses thoughtful theories on the subject. According to the map found on Peter's website, they are the First Nations and Kachina Lines. They are of Native American origin.

First Nations is a tragic path of spirit travel. It falls over sacred sites, locations of massacres, and battles. Memories of the past move along this path, and as they do, pull or attract similar memories. It represents the white man's persecution of other races. This is a line of death, blood, and tragedy.

The Kachina Ley or Kachina Highway extends from the Baja Peninsula to the Cape Breton Peninsula. It is a spirit line connecting sacred mountains both above ground and in the water. The Kachina starts where the Hopi Indian gods (Kachinas) reside underground, the San Francisco Mountains. It contains good and evil gods and represents historical events and things in nature.

North American ley lines

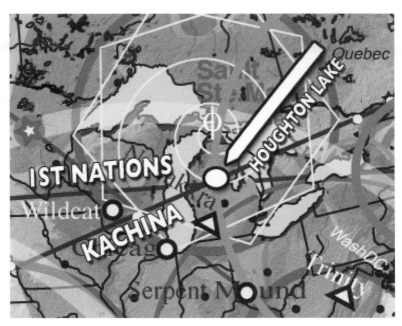

Two major ley lines, First Nation and Kachina, intersect in Houghton Lake.

With these two lines intersecting in Houghton Lake, we wondered what spiritual or tragic connection there was to Roscommon County. Here's where we returned to historical research.

Before the white man came to Roscommon County, it was home to large Ottawa and Chippewa settlements. Numerous burial sites and Indian mounds were located throughout the region. Today, much of Houghton Lake is built over these decimated sites. In the 1800s the Native American tribes were tragically forced to leave the land they had called home for so many generations. The two lines meet in Houghton Lake because of the sad and spiritual connection to Native Americans.

Our investigation at the Anchor Inn begins to make sense using the ley line theory. First, Ronda mentioned that a lot of her guests have shared stories about paranormal activity in and surrounding Houghton Lake. Could it be the ley lines are holding the spirits as well as past memories traveling along this invisible highway of earth energy?

We then considered the strange and frightening images Ronda's daughter Miranda and other people have seen. If the ominous shadows were real and not the result of over-active imaginations, could these be travelers on the highway? Beings that occasionally pass through the veil to our dimension.

Lastly, we reviewed the abundance of voices and murmurs that seemed random or unintelligible at the inn. It reminded us of three or four other investigations where unusually large amounts of EVP were captured, such as the Whitney Restaurant in Detroit. We soon discovered each location had ley lines running through. In fact, Michigan is a hot bed of energy, according to ley line theorists, because of the Great Lakes and large quantity of inland lakes.

Our investigation at the Anchor Inn was without a doubt different than many. It was difficult to find any records or documents to corroborate stories; yet, we collected an abundance of evidence. Ronda and her family have had numerous experiences.

Since our visit to the inn, others have investigated with minimal or no evidence. Is it possible that the ley lines along with unusually large solar flares created the perfect storm for paranormal activity?

Story Eight:
Carriage House B&B

5967 Andersonville Rd,
Waterford, MI 48329
248-623-0025

Investigative Team: Clarkston Haunted
Investigative Paranormal Seekers (CHIPS)

Password: fer1893

PEOPLE DRIVING DOWN ANDERSONVILLE ROAD may miss one of Waterford's historic treasures, the Carriage House Bed and Breakfast. At night, with inside lights casting their amber glow across the yard, it appears warm and homey. In spite of its inviting appearance, rumors persist of its haunting.

These tales of the supernatural were brought to our attention by C.H.I.P.S., a paranormal team based in Clarkston. Team founders, Robert and Sharon Dowd, had investigated the residence on several occasions collecting enough personal experiences and evidence to capture our attention.

A waning crescent moon sent its dim threads of light across the night sky as we turned up the narrow driveway to the old home. Members of the C.H.I.P.S. team were already there and beginning to setup equipment for the night's hunt.

Bob and Shari opened the back door and called out to us. The chilled November air turned their breath into faint swirling clouds. Pulling our jackets close, we quickly entered the house to warm up. It was zestfully cold inside. For a moment we wondered if the spirits had sucked all the heat from the home. If so, this place was crazy with ghosts. But no, the heat simply had not been turned on.

Shari and Bob, the founders of C.H.I.P.S.

As the home began to warm, Bob and Shari took us on a tour sharing both its history and haunting. It is said the home was built circa 1865, although early records seem to indicate it was built before then. Land maps show some kind of structure on the property as far back as 1837.

We'll likely never know who the very first residents were. Back in the 1830s, Waterford was just a vast, unbroken wilderness. Only a handful of hearty souls inhabited the land, and no ownership documents were kept. Even Detroit was referred to as a small French town.

The house was surprisingly small for today's standards, but very typical of the era. It consisted of a kitchen and main dining/gathering room. There was a half story above it that likely contained a sleeping loft. In the early 1870s, additions were added that included the first floor parlor and two bedrooms upstairs. Around the turn of the century, the home was expanded to its current size.

Bob and Shari explained that, for some time, strange phenomena has been reported throughout the house. Footsteps in the dining room and the sound of chairs scraping along the wood floor of the parlor have been heard.

Bob believes he has a certain amount of sensitivity and told us he had sensed a woman standing at the top of the stairs. He has also seen a man wearing a suit and hat smoking in the parlor. More shadowy apparitions have been reported on the second floor along with disembodied voices and the sound of doors opening and closing.

It is believed at least one of the spirits who remain is that of Emily Tilden. She and her husband William were the first owners of the home. Emily's heritage is quite fascinating. Her parents, Ferdinand Williams and Phebe Cook, were among the earliest settlers to the area.

Ferdinand Williams was a rogue, born to a privileged Detroit family. He wasn't born in the wilderness yet the wilderness called him. Ferdinand loved nature, solitude, hunting, and working the land. He preferred being away from populations and society in general, much to the ire of his father John Williams, one of Michigan's elite citizens.

John Williams was an early political leader in Detroit's history and became its first mayor in 1824. Many attribute the rapid growth of Detroit and the surrounding areas to John for his political ambitions and keen sense of business. He must have been somewhat disappointed when his well-educated son, destined to follow in his footsteps, went off into the wilderness of Oakland County instead.

For Phebe, the wilderness of Oakland County was nothing new. She had been raised in the wild timberland of western New York. A strong, nurturing woman, Phebe held the family together during her husband's many absences. In the late 1820s, the couple settled in the rugged, unbroken wilderness of the area now known as Waterford.

According to one historical account, during the vicious Black Hawk wars, Phebe was left with her children while her husband went for supplies. During his absence, news of an Indian uprising and mass murder of white settlers reached her. In fear for her children's lives, the young mother locked the cabin and hid under bushes near the bank of the lake. There she kept the children calm, quiet, and safe waiting for Ferdinand's return. Her fear grew as daylight waned and he had not yet appeared. Had her husband fallen victim to Black Hawk's rage? We can only imagine her profound relief when she finally heard his voice calling her name.

Not much is known of Phebe's third child, Emily. We do know she was married at the age of twenty-two to William Tilden. The Tildens, like the Williams family, were early settlers to the area. Emily had known William Tilden most of her life, and their marriage seemed an inevitable union. After the marriage, she and William moved into the house that is now the Carriage Inn. Three years later they had their first and only child, Ferdinand.

Life changed for the young couple in 1862 when William was drafted into Michigan's 15th Infantry to fight with the northern armies in the Civil War. He bravely fought in the Siege of Corinth, Mississippi, and took ill shortly thereafter. Disease ended his life and Emily was left alone to raise their son.

Several years later Emily married a carriage maker, Lorenzo Streeter, whose shop was across the road from her home. Here's where things become a little murky. We weren't able to find a valid marriage record and are puzzled that she kept her last name Tilden. In fact, both her tombstone and death record use the Tilden name, without reference to Streeter. What her true relationship to Lorenzo was may never be known.

A year after Emily's death, in 1878, Lorenzo remarried and left town. Her son Ferdinand remained at the family home. It was around this time his grandmother, Phebe, came to live with him. Phebe remained with Ferdinand even after he married and cared for the couple's first child, a boy named after his father.

Ferdinand's career as a druggist frequently took him to Detroit. In fact he had two recorded residences, one in Detroit and the family home in Waterford. Much like his grandmother, Ferdinand wanted to keep the family together. When he and his wife couldn't be there, Grandma Phebe would be, and she was trusted completely. As the years passed, the young boy grew a strong attachment to his grandmother.

The Carriage House Circa 1865

Phebe had overcome many personal and physical challenges in her life. Being a strong, determined woman, she got past them all. However, an injury sustained at the age of eighty-four would ultimately lead to her downfall. An infection set in. The local doctor treated the wound as best he could, but it worsened. Gangrene set in and rapidly spread. She succumbed from the infection in 1892. Although records don't say, it is most likely she died at home. Her body, like her daughter Emily and those who may have died in the home before, reposed in the parlor prior to burial. In those days, that was the custom.

Phebe's death was a great loss to her family. Ferdinand was shocked. He had expected a full recovery. After all, his grandmother had been through much greater challenges in her life. As difficult as it was for Ferdinand to accept, for his young son just six years old, it was an emotionally devastating blow.

After Phebe's death, Ferdinand and his wife maintained both their Waterford and Detroit homes. Why he kept both homes is not clear. Maybe the old homestead had sentimental value for him. He may also have kept it for purely practical reasons. It was a convenient place to stay while he worked in Waterford. Of course he may have kept it for all of those reasons. We will never know.

Sadly, the greatest challenge to Ferdinand and his wife, Allie, was yet to be faced.

The winter of 1893, Michigan, like much of the U.S., was hit with a series of deadly diseases. Tuberculosis, diphtheria, whooping cough, scarlet fever, and measles swept through the towns.

That year there was an unusually high outbreak of scarlet fever. An adult's natural immune system made them fairly resilient to the disease. If contracted, it was generally very mild. Tragically, it was often deadly to those under the age of ten. Parents pensively watched their children for the first signs of a sore throat, chills, and fever—all precursors to scarlet fever's terrible red rash.

Dreaded "Quarantine" signs became a sad but common sight posted on the doors of neighbors and friends. It was a frightening indicator that insidious disease was present in the home. Those inside remained isolated from the outside world. How alone and frightened they must have been.

Scarlet fever was most often passed on through coughing, sneezing, and breathing out the bacteria. What many didn't realize is that the bacteria could also be transmitted through milk. Dairy farmers would milk their cows not realizing they carried the deadly disease. Coughing near the milk or even touching it with contaminated hands would embed the bacteria. The infected milk would be distributed and consumed by unsuspecting, innocent children.

With Detroit being highly populated and virulent diseases sweeping the city, Ferdinand and Allie thought it would be safer for young Ferdinand, then seven years old, to leave town. That winter and spring the young lad spent as much time as possible away from the city surrounded by the fresh air of the country.

It was early May 1893. The scent of spring blossoms filled the air, and the ever-present fear of disease began to lift. New cases of scarlet fever were fewer and fewer. Ferdinand and his wife were pleased their son thrived in the country air and farm-fresh produce from the area and breathed a sigh of relief that their young son remained strong and happy.

One morning, after breakfast, Allie sent her young son out to play. He came in not long after claiming to not feel well. She put him to bed. A few hours later she came in to check and, to her horror, he had a raging fever, his small body raked with chills.

A pharmacist for many years, when Ferdinand heard the news he immediately feared the worst. It was scarlet fever.

The lad was taken to a Detroit hospital for better medical care, but treatments failed. On May 14, 1893, nearly one year to the month of Grandma Phebe's passing, little Ferdinand died. The Tildens were devastated.

Years turned into decades. The Tildens eventually sold the home. It changed owners several times, eventually purchased by Richard and Mary Sies in the 1950s . After his wife's passing, Mr. Sies remained in the home until his death on a cold February day in 1993. His body was discovered resting in his favorite parlor chair. Years later, the home was purchased by The Carriage House Partners, its current owners.

·After the tour, we asked Bob and Shari what was their most compelling piece of recorded evidence. Both smiled, looked at each other, and in unison said, "Seth." It was their clearest EVP to date, recorded in an upstairs bedroom. Without a last name, it's impossible to know who Seth may be. However, Phebe's father and Emily's grandfather was Seth Cook. Perhaps tonight we would discover who uttered those words.

With the tour completed, the investigation began. The group was divided into two teams. I went upstairs with two members of CHIPS, Steve and Maggie, to run an audio session in the Tilden Room. We were not there more than a few minutes when our first EVP was recorded.

It came during the time Steve and Maggie were talking about their previous investigation here. Maggie mentioned the energy in the home and this room was different tonight.

"The first time I came here... we pulled up and as we were walking up to the house I just had this feeling of sadness and dread. When I got in the house, it got worse. Then, when I came up here, especially this room, it just didn't feel right, like something bad had happened."

The Tilden Room seemed active that night

The EVP came just before she began speaking. The exact words repeated as soon as she finished. It sounded like a male voice that said, "Shut her up." The spirit energy seemed to not only anticipate her words but didn't like what she had to say after. The remainder of our time in the Tilden Room was quiet and uneventful. If there had been a spirit, it was gone.

Groups rotated throughout the house for the next few hours. It was around 9:40 p.m. Robert's team was running a session in the basement and Shari was running another upstairs.

Bev and I settled in the parlor. After a few minutes, Bev left to place another stationary audio recorder on the second floor.

For a moment, I was alone in the parlor. Faint tendrils of light crept through the front windows from outside street lamps. Their incandescent glow cast long shadows across the silent room. In the eerie stillness, I began to ask questions.

"I understand the Tildens were here. Can you tell me who Seth is? Who is Seth?" It was then the K2 hit. Its lights flashed quickly then quieted. A possible response?

I repositioned my video camera on the K2 meter as my questions continued to focus on the name, Seth. "Do you know Seth? Is he with us?" Unknown to me at the time, an EVP was recorded. The voice was flat, unemotional, dead, and said, "Never here."

Kat waiting after K2 responses

We had thought the "Seth" EVP recorded by C.H.I.P.S. may have been referring to Phebe's father, Seth Cook. Did this mean her father was never at the home? If not, then why was the name picked up? The answer may be very simple. Could Phebe, as she lay in delirium, the poison from gangrene spreading throughout her body, call out the name of her father? Is that what the C.H.I.P.S. team recorded?

It was not long after that Bev re-entered the room. I told her about the K2 hitting just minutes ago. However, before I could finish the sentence the K2 spiked again. This time the lights went full red.

As it would turn out, it was then another EVP was recorded. This was a different voice. Raspy, low it said, "My name... can you hear me... Lorenzo."

As mentioned earlier, Lorenzo Streeter was said to be Emily Tilden's second husband. He was responsible for the additions to the home in the 1870s, including the parlor where this EVP was captured.

Bev checking equipment

Lorenzo enjoyed working with his hands and was a skilled builder. He placed his heart and soul into his work. Could his spirit remain attached?

On a previous investigation, Bob reported hearing wood scraping on the floor of the parlor. At the time, he thought it sounded like chairs moving. We wonder if what Bob heard was Lorenzo at work.

Sometime near midnight, the entire group gathered in the parlor. Bob and Shari wanted to test out one of their new ideas for investigation. A few days before, Bob had purchased a plasma globe. You've likely seen one. They're often found in toy and novelty stores. It's a clear glass or Lucite orb filled with various gases, most commonly neon. When plugged in, electrical charges are set off and multi-colored fingers of electricity bounce in erratic patterns. Bob was hoping the electricity would either draw spirits to it or visually react if a spirit drew near, just as it would when a hand is placed on it.

Bob and Shari's son, Nathan, checking on the plasma globe.

We thought it was a unique idea and were eager to see if it would work. The globe was placed in the center of the room. Next, audio and video recorders and EMF meters were set strategically around to cast an electronic net.

With everyone and everything in place, Bob and Shari began the session. Their questions were directed toward members of the Williams, Tilden, Streeter, or Sies families. The first thirty minutes were uneventful.

Since members of Emily Tilden's family were French, Nate decided to try an experiment. He used the voice-activated language application on his smartphone to translate English into French. Unfortunately, it did not result in a response. However, we do believe this is an interesting approach to use in future investigations.

After our session in the parlor, it was getting late. The team decided to wrap up for the evening. During this time, I placed my audio recorder running on the kitchen table. To our surprise, we discovered it had captured one of our best EVPs of the night.

Sometimes the best evidence is collected when you least expect it. This EVP, a child's voice, clearly said, "I got chills from the milk."

Initially we thought it a curious statement until we recalled little Ferdinand and his tragic death in 1893 from scarlet fever. One of the first symptoms of the disease is a sore throat followed by chills and a high fever. Milk was considered a common home remedy believed to coat the throat and soothe the pain. His mother may very well have given him milk for that purpose. Shortly after that the chills and fever began.

Did the little boy, not understanding his condition, think the milk was responsible for his chills? He may also have heard his parents talking about scarlet fever being transmitted through milk. Did the lad then assume the milk he drank was responsible for his illness and chills?

The Carriage House has seen nearly 150 years of life. It remains a complex mystery with a haunting that includes both residual and intelligent energies. Exactly who remains or why is part of that mystery and part of its fascination.

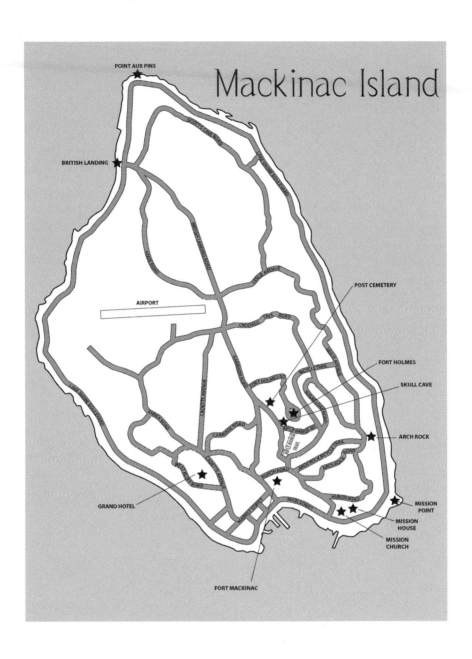

Mackinac Island

POINT AUX PINS

BRITISH LANDING

POST CEMETERY

AIRPORT

FORT HOLMES

SKULL CAVE

ARCH ROCK

GRAND HOTEL

MISSION POINT

MISSION HOUSE

MISSION CHURCH

FORT MACKINAC

Introduction:
A Haunted Weekend on
Mackinac Island

THE BEGINNING

"IT'S HAUNTED." THE OLD MAN said. "All of it. The whole island."

It was 1990. Bev and I were working on the kick-off book of our first series, *Michigan Vacation Guide*. Part of our initial research required attending a public Native American Power-Wow in St. Ignace. We were listening to a storyteller share tales of Mackinac Island when the old man, sitting next to us, whispered those words.

He had dark, piercing eyes that looked out from a face worn and withered with age yet still strong. His russet-colored skin, high cheekbones, and strong facial features spoke of his ancestry.

His name was George. He'd been born and raised on Mackinac Island and spent a good part of his eighty-plus years there. George said he was mostly Anishinaabe (Ojibwa) although he grudgingly admitted to having some French and English blood in him.

George had explored every foot of the island in his youth claiming to know it better than anyone else. I wish we'd had our audio or video recorder to capture his stories. Instead, what he told us was jotted down on a crumpled piece of paper Bev found at the bottom of her purse and the rest kept to memory.

His People once considered the island most sacred. It was home to Gitche Manitou, the "Great Spirit." Indian tribes from all around would gather at the island to make offerings. Tribal chiefs were buried there using sacred ceremonics. Indeed, it was a Holy Place.

The land was revered for hundreds of years until the first French explorers came. Other Europeans followed as the island became a fur-trading hub. Then Christians ministers arrived building missions to teach the Indians *civilized* ways and their religion. Eventually the British and Americans claimed Mackinac Island as their own.

Slowly Native Americans lost their way and their land. Ancient, sacred burial sites found throughout the island were desecrated, and the remains of their ancestors were dug up, thrown away, destroyed, or simply forgotten without ceremony. It was an abomination. It was *civilization* and is part of Mackinac Island's history.

According to George, to desecrate the remains of sacred ancestors is to ask for trouble. Spirits cannot rest when their bodies were so disrespectfully removed from sacred ground. Spiritual retribution would be expected.

What followed on the island were battles. Many deaths. Tragedies filled with fighting, horrible disease, greed, and corruption.

Bev and I asked if he thought it was the curse from restless souls and the Great Spirit or just the way of man?

The old man simply shrugged. He didn't know, but he swore the acts of the past had left their mark on the island and that ghosts, many nameless spirits, still roamed. Not all were Indian; some were white, but their presence remained. He believed they wander, lost, seeking release from this earth to their spiritual home.

During his earlier years on the island, George claimed to have seen many such spirits. Some were as solid and clear as a living person while others appeared faded, quickly passing on some unknown journey. Sometimes it was just a feeling in the air, he said, a tingling of the skin that signaled their energy was near.

We remember him telling us, "On a calm, still day when the wind gusts, listen, watch. They're with you then. As fleeting and sightless as the wind but as real as the oxygen we breathe."

His tales of ghostly specters held our attention and remain with us to this day. It was one of the reasons we chose to begin our own paranormal journey on Mackinac Island, the land of Gitche Manitou. The "Great Spirit." We wanted to see for ourselves if the ghostly stories of Mackinac Island were true.

We began a series of ghost hunts exploring many areas of the island, bringing a group of guest investigators with us. With each investigation, more and more evidence of paranormal phenomena was recorded. Even on back roads, miles from the busy downtown district and historic buildings, evidence was captured. George would have nodded his head and said, "I told you so."

The following chapters are the stories of our investigations on the island. They are for George and all those who have felt the wind blow on a calm, still day.

OUR ARRIVAL: The History and
Folklore of Mackinac Island.

It was the first weekend in October when we ran our first investigation. The sky was a deep blue. A few white, puffy clouds scattered above reflected brighter with the warm sun. Temperatures that weekend would be unusually warm with highs reaching the mid-70s. It didn't get much better than that for an outdoor investigation.

Bev and I would first be meeting up with Todd Clements, author of *Haunts of Mackinac.* Todd also operates a popular haunted tour company on the island. He is one of the go-to guys for island history and stories of ghostly phenomena and would be helping us with the weekend hunt. After our meeting with Todd, we'd meet the group of people who would be joining in this weekend's ghost hunting adventure.

The jet boat ride from St. Ignace to the island has always been one of our favorite parts of island trips. Guests can choose an upper deck, open-air seat or stay in the more protected lower level. It was such a warm day, we decided on the upper deck.

It wasn't long before the boat took off. The calm, warm day turned into a wild ride; motors kicked into high gear and we sped to the island. Wind tore at our hair and clothes, and spray from the lake kicked up covering us in a fine mist. Hmm. It had suddenly gotten much, much colder but was still absolutely fantastic.

As the boat made its way across the strait, our eyes scanned the horizon taking in the incredible deep blue of the lake. Our boat sped past the Mackinac Bridge. Although seen many times before, the bridge still presented an amazing sight, especially on this brilliant day. Its massive support beams towered impressively toward the sky, their appearance pure white.

In the distance we saw the island now called Mackinac. Originally it was Michilimackinac, a name that some say came from the Ottawa/Chippewa Indians. The words Mi-she means *tremendous in size;* and mi-ki-nock, translates to a m*ud turtle.* Thus Michilimackinac translates to "large turtle" island.

Mackinac Island

Although the island does indeed look like the back of a giant tortoise shell rising from the waters, some Native Americans disagree with the more contemporary version of this story. They claim the island was named after an ancient tribe of Indians that existed on the land long before the Ottawa arrived. This small, independent tribe called themselves the Mi-shi-ne-macki-naw-go. They became good friends of the Ottawa people and shared a mutual respect for each other.

As tradition tells, one day the Mi-shi-ne-macki-naw-go were attacked by a roaming band of Seneca, and all but two members of the tribe, a young man and woman, were killed. The couple saved themselves by taking refuge in an island cave until the fighting was over. They eventually made their way back to their friends, the Ottawa, and told the story of the massacre. According to this story, the Ottawa named the island Mi-shi-ne-macki-naw-go as a monument to the existence of their friends. From that came the name Michilimackinac.

The legend continues that the young man and woman, last members of the Mi-shi-ne-macki-naw-go tribe, left the island. They eventually settled in the wilderness of Lower Michigan near Pine Lake in Charlevoix County. There they lived happily, rejecting

other human life. They had ten children, all boys. It is said the
Mi-shi-ne-macki-naw-go still roam the remote areas around Pine
Lake as supernatural beings. Over the decades there have been
continuing reports of unknown footsteps in the woods and trails
and fleeting visions of Indian braves wandering the remaining
areas of wilderness, but that's another story for another book.

We kept our eyes on the impressive white building on a hill
to the left of center, the Grand Hotel. One of the island's oldest
and most famous, it has been the site of several movies including
the memorable *Somewhere In Time*. It has also been featured in
several books.

The Grand Hotel

There are rumors the Grand is one of the island's most haunted
locations. The rumors are yet to be proven. The Grand does not
permit paranormal investigations. Until they do, stories of its
haunting remain just that—stories. Of course, if you want to
reserve a room for a few hundred dollars a night, you may be able
to find out for yourself if those stories are true.

The Grand Hotel was not our destination this weekend. Mission
Point Resort, on the southeastern side of the island, was. This lovely
hotel rests on spacious, beautifully landscaped grounds along the
lakeshore and offers one of most scenic views on the island.

Downtown Mackinac Island

Bev and I arrived a little after 2 p.m. Stepping from the boat we were immediately transported to the nineteenth century. The clip-clop of hooves echoed down the streets as horse-driven carriages and wagons took people or supplies to various island destinations. Quiet laughter could be heard from folks leisurely walking by. Rows of bicycles instead of cars lined the streets.

Not a single car was seen nor the sound of a churning motors heard. Motorized vehicles are not permitted on the island, at least not from spring to fall.

As the porter searched out our luggage, we stepped onto the sidewalk. Beautifully preserved, historic buildings lined the main street, each looking very much like they have for over a century. Hotels, restaurants, fudge shops, and small gift boutiques open their doors to welcome island visitors. The serenity of the island and its history has drawn visitors to it for well over 150 years.

After a short carriage ride, we arrived at Mission Point where we'd be meeting up with Todd Clements to go over our plans and identify key areas to target for our outdoor investigations. After that we'd gather our group together to share the details of the weekend investigations. What happened during our series of daytime ghost hunting adventures on Mackinac Island follows.

Story Nine:
The Ruins of Fort Holmes

Mackinac Island, Michigan
Assisted by: Todd Clements, Haunts of Mackinac

Password: rfh1012

THERE REALLY WERE NO GHOST stories associated with Fort Holmes, at least not the first couple of times we investigated the old ruins. In fact, to the best of our knowledge, we were the first group to actually run a formal paranormal investigation here.

Fort Holmes is situated at the highest point of Mackinac Island and is nothing at all like the well-known Fort Mackinac less than a mile beneath it. Little remains of the original fortress except for earthworks and the main gate. Even the gate is not part of the original fort but was reconstructed during a 1930's renovation project.

The original fort was built by the British in 1812 and named Fort George, after the King of England. It was primarily a defensive fortress, referred to as a redoubt. It was built to protect Fort Mackinac against the U.S. military and was the bulwark of British defenses in the 1814 Battle of Mackinac Island.

During the 1914 battle, a heroic young American officer, Major Andrew H. Holmes, was shot and killed. When the Americans finally regained control of the island after the 1815 treaty, they renamed the fort after Major Holmes.

Fort Holmes was eventually abandoned by the Americans and fell into disrepair. During the Great Depression of the 1930s, the Civilian Conservation Corps (CCC) came in to reconstruct it. For those unfamiliar with the CCC, it was a government sponsored work welfare program giving jobs to the unskilled and unemployed.

Through the hard efforts of these individuals, the fort was meticulously restored using original blueprints. Unfortunately, not long after it was restored, a fire swept through damaging much of the log structures. In time, the fort was again forgotten. As mentioned earlier, all that remains today are earthworks and the main gate.

Although no soldiers were killed at Fort Holmes, there is at least one tragedy that may have left its mark. It was August 1906 when New York newlyweds Benjamin and Katherine Frankle came to the island on their honeymoon.

Their first full day on Mackinac Island was a beautiful, sunny Saturday morning. Filled with excitement, the couple decided to venture up to Fort Holmes to check out the scenic view and explore the old fort. In those days there was a thirty-foot observation tower on the grounds. Katherine and Benjamin decided to climb to the top. At that moment when Katherine turned to go down, she tripped and lost her footing. Her hand slipped from the rail, and young Katherine tragically fell to her death.

Fort Holmes showing the old observation tower.

Benjamin was horrified and guilt-ridden, blaming himself for failing to keep his new bride safe. It was a guilt he carried with him to the grave. We wondered if the spirit of Katherine and Benjamin remained locked to the last place they shared together.

The next morning came quickly. Bev and I met our eager group and boarded the waiting carriages. The horse-driven buggies meandered through the downtown district, past the Grand Hotel, taking a turn from there on an upward trail. It was a slow go. The road to Fort Holmes is indeed steep and, although some walk or bicycle to the top, on this morning we were grateful to have the horses take that burden from us.

That time of year the island was especially beautiful. Fall colors were at peak and the wooded trails were filled with bright reds, oranges, and yellows. If we thought the trails were scenic, we'd be even more amazed at the top.

At the time we were there, the view from Fort Holmes' bluff was really indescribable, of immense beauty, and brilliant colors in every direction. A dense covering of trees at the bottom appeared like plump, colorful broccoli flowing out and ending at the deep blue of the lake. Incredible. Even if this trip resulted in recording no paranormal evidence, the view alone would make our time here worthwhile.

We eventually returned to the focus of our travels, the investigation. Everyone broke into small teams and took positions both inside and outside the earthwork. Many carried EMF meters and audio recorders. We literally had the fort grounds surrounded. If any electromagnetic fields passed through, they would be identified.

Kat settles in to begin the first EVP session.

Idle chatter ceased; the group quieted as our EVP session began. I started by calling out to Katherine Frankle. "I know there was sadness here. I know there was death here." Pausing briefly, I continued. "Is Katherine here? If you're here can you come up to the silver box (indicating my audio recorder). That will record your voice. You were here Katie, do you remember? You fell."

Quiet settled around us, an uncanny stillness. There was not a trace of wind, which seemed unusual considering we were sitting in a very exposed location at the highest point on the island. If there was a breath of wind anywhere, it would be here. Yet, not even the leaves at the top-most portions of tree branches stirred.

Bev spoke to Katherine, "You fell on your honeymoon. Such a sad time. Katherine, are you here?"

The stillness remained. We continued our questions for several minutes, but on this quiet afternoon, if their spirits were here, they remained elusive.

We then turned to the Ojibwa people. For centuries, Ojibwa and Chippewa were a strong presence on the island. I began the session by speaking their language, hoping that may open a channel of communication.

Sitting crossed legged on the still-damp grass, I opened my note pad where I had jotted down a few Ojibwa words. Clearly not fluent in the language, I hoped my mispronunciation of words would still be understood by lingering native spirits.

I began with a greeting, "Boozoo." A word derivative of the French "Boujou" obviously influenced by early French traders. With no response, I tried the more traditional Ojibwa greeting, "Aanii."

I glanced at the teams surrounding the grounds to see if any were indicating an EMF fluctuation. Nothing.

I continued my badly broken Ojibwa for the next fifteen minutes. From there we turned to the British and American soldiers. As things continued to remain quiet, we decided to stir up a bit of controversy. I spoke out suggesting the American commander who allowed the island to be taken over so easily by the British was not a capable leader. Although the event itself didn't connect to Fort Holmes, we were hoping any existing spirit energy may recall the incident and react.

After that question we again waited in silence. The bright sun shed rays of warmth around us as we were lulled into a calm, nearly meditative state. It was then I noticed the first stirring of wind, a gentle brush of air that lightly pulled at my hair and shuffled the grass at my feet.

"K2!" Bev called out.

Seconds later, the team standing on the rim of the earthworks across from Bev signaled an EMF spike. Were the spikes just passing waves of energy that flow through our atmosphere or could they be signaling the start of a paranormal event?

I called out, "We're here to talk with anyone from Fort Holmes, British or American." We would later discover an EVP had been recorded that said, "American. I'm here."

Unfortunately, at that exact time we could hear a family coming to the fort grounds. They were not with our group, simply visitors coming to check out the area. We settled back and waited until the family left and continued our session. It seemed whatever may have caused the brief spike was gone.

Our questions then turned to the laborers of the CCC who had once worked so hard at restoring the old fort. Again, it was frustratingly quiet.

Time was slipping away. We would have to wrap this portion of the investigation soon. In a last attempt, I resumed our broken Ojibwa. My words telling Native spirits I was from the tribe of Tedsen. I repeated the word a few times hoping that would elicit a response.

That's when I again heard Bev call out, "K2." She raised her hand signaling for the group to remain silent. I repeated the words, louder this time. Bev again signaled. This time it was a powerful K2 burst. All five lights flashed.

Moving towards Bev, I repeated the words, "In-doe-den. In-doe-den," hoping the spirits would respond by telling me their tribe's name. With those words, the K2 lights shot full red and began flashing wildly.

A very strong energy had settled around us. I could feel it. Hair on the back of my arms rose, and there was that slightly dizzy sensation I get when EMF levels are high. The energy was also affecting sound on the video recorder's audio as static interference began.

Team members gather around Bev as her K2 meter responds to questions.

Bev took my video recorder and focused it on the K2, "Were you here before the white man?" The lights flashed wildly as the static grew stronger on the camera's audio.

"Is this your land?" The K2 lights became a frenzy of flashes as the static on audio turned into a solid hum.

If this was a spirit, it was very agitated, excited—too excited to get a consistent response. "Okay. Calm down. Calm down," I whispered.

The lights slowly stilled, but within a moment they had returned to their frantic flickering. "Calm down. It's okay. We hear you," I continued.

To our surprise, the wild flashing stopped. Bev and I glanced at each other in a silent question. What did we have here? I sent an Ojibwa greeting, "Boozoo." To that, the K2 lights responded.

Bev resumed her questions. "Were you here before the white man?" Full red on the K2. Again Bev and I exchange glances. Were we communicating with a Native American spirit?

Then the most amazing thing happened. Bev's K2 went flat, the lights darkened. A second later the team next to us raised a hand. Another hit. Bev and I watched as, in succession, each team raised their hand or called out as EMF meters spiked one after the other after the other. A swirling force of energy was literally sweeping the grounds of Fort Holmes until it amazingly circled around toward us. It was then Bev's K2 began flashing. In all our many investigation, Bev and I had never encountered such a strong, controlled, sweeping EMF flow.

I left to check on the other teams as Bev continued, "Are you Ojibwa?" The K2 hit.

"Are you a man?" Another hit. "Are you a *young* man?" Lights flashed again.

Bev, uncertain how a young Ojibwe male could understand English, asked "How is it you can understand me?" This time the K2 remained unresponsive. After a few moments she asked, "Can you understand me?" The K2 came back to life, flashing several times. Perhaps the spirit didn't know why he could understand what Bev way saying, he just did.

For the next fifteen minutes, the K2 continued what seemed to be responses to questions. Based on what just happened, the spirit was that of a young Ojibwa male. He was not alone. There were other spirits with him. That may well have been true since K2 responses swept through our group with every Ojibwa word spoken.

Bev, however, seemed to be getting the most consistently strong responses. As the other EMF hits quieted, the group gathered around Bev listening and watching as the K2 continued to respond to her questions. Eventually the responses grew weaker. It seemed whatever energy had been near was leaving us. It had been an hour, and we needed to head on to our next investigation site.

I thanked the spirits for their response, "Migwetch." Todd Clements, wearing headphones and listening for real-time EVPs looked up. He'd heard a response.

Rewinding, we took turns listening. Indeed, Todd was right. There was a faint yet obvious reciprocating, "Migwetch." The voice was male, and the accent sounded Native American, perhaps Ojibwa.

After final audio review, back at our office, we would discover something we didn't originally notice. The wind. It was still until the crazy K2 session. Occasionally, there were gusts so strong they blocked out our words. Now, of course, we have to consider the possibility natural energy from the wind may have somehow affected K2 and Mel-Meter readings. However, we did capture a few EVPs during this time, which would reinforce the existence of spirit energy.

In addition to the "Migwetch," we picked up two additional EVPs. Although we could not understand what they said, the tone and accent of the words did sound Native American. You can hear these EVPs in our Secret Room.

We were not finished with our investigation of Fort Holmes, returning the following year. As before, we divided the group into teams that surrounded the fort grounds. Although our second investigation was quieter than the first, we did have an area of response. A small team was positioned in the same area of the grounds where Bev had been the previous year, just to the left, at the bottom of the earthen wall.

It was about the same time of day, 1:00 p.m., when the EMF fluctuations began. The first EVP captured was Native American. Again, we couldn't understand the word, but the tone and accent certainly sounded Native American. This time, the Native American influence was just a brief moment. In its place were fort soldiers.

Some time later, Maria believed they were getting responses from a fort soldier. She asked, "Soldier, can you tell us your name and rank." The EVP captured was surprisingly clear and said, "Can you see me?"

Bev and I were still wondering about Katherine and Benjamin Frankle, the newlyweds from New York who were tragically separated when Katherine fell to her death from the Fort Holmes Observation tower. Although several EVPs had been captured suggesting soldiers and Native American spirits roamed the grounds, nothing had been recorded to suggest the spirit of Katherine and Benjamin remained.

I lagged behind as our group made their way to the next location. Alone now, I stood silently in the center of Fort Holmes surrounded by the remnants of its earthworks. A K2 held in one hand and an audio recorder in the other, I called the name of Katherine and Benjamin. It was at the mention of Benjamin's name that the K2 hit. Not strong, just a flutter of green and yellow lights. Calling his name again gave me yet another weak K2 response.

Was Katherine's husband near? Was Benjamin finally attempting to communicate? I quietly asked one last question, "Why do you stay?" I scanned the surrounding area listening intently for something, anything that might indicate a response. Regretfully, there was nothing. I turned and quickly made my way to the others now well down the path

What we would not discover until later is there had been a response. Very quiet, so quiet headphones needed to be pressed against the ear to block out any extraneous noise. But it was there, a male voice. His answer had been short, simple. "Kathy."

Story Ten:
The Old Post Cemetery

Assisted By: Todd Clements

Password: mpcfall

N O ONE IS EXACTLY CERTAIN how old the Post is, but we do know it dates back at least 150 years. The earliest headstones were damaged by the island's harsh weather, and many of the early records are lost to time. However old it is, one thing is certain, ghost stories related to the old Post are plentiful.

As Todd shared with us, one of the cemetery's most famous ghosts is that of Crying Mary. Her weeping image is reported hovering and weeping over the headstones of her dead children. In addition to Crying Mary, the apparitions of old fort soldiers and even children have been seen wandering.

Our group quietly entered, respectful of the hollowed grounds we now walked. To the right were row after row of tombstones simply marked "Unknown Soldier"—a reminder of the many lost souls whose names are forgotten.

We broke into two sub-teams. Bev took one team while I took the other. Time passed slowly. Weeping Mary didn't show up on this warm afternoon nor was there an appearance from spectral soldiers or ghostly children. In fact, our thirty minutes were unremarkable and very quiet.

First EVP session begins

A few team members had settled on a short wall near the back resting before the trek to our next investigation site, about a mile away. Just a few feet from me was an "Unknown Soldier" tombstone. I knelt before it and began one last EVP session.

The video camera's battery was running low and would need to be changed before we moved to the last location. For now, I simply turned it off wanting to conserve whatever charge was left should an interesting event begin.

Introducing myself and pointing to the audio recorder on the ground, I asked the spirit to speak into it if they would like to communicate. Thinking I was too close to the tombstone, I backed away saying, "Maybe I'm too close." It was after that an EVP was captured, "No, you're not." Whoever lies beneath this tombstone may never be known but, whoever it was, their spirit seemed to see and hear me, perhaps wanting me to stay close.

It was not long after that EVP I noticed the wind again. Its sound rustled through the treetops, descending around us before quickly dissipating. Stillness returned.

Kat begins another session before the grave of an unknown soldier.

There was something about the sudden, strong gust that reminded me of George, the old Ojibwa we had met years before at the St. Ignace Pow-Wow. When talking of the spirits he'd said, "On a calm, still day when the wind gusts, listen. Watch. They're with you then. As fleeting and sightless as the wind but as real as the oxygen we breathe."

Returning my attention to the Unknown Soldier's tombstone, I asked, "Is your message in the wind?" That's when the first K2 hit occurred. An investigator seated on the half-wall signaled the spike. I got up, flipping my video camera on and settled beside her.

"Were you telling me you do in fact speak in the wind... that your voice is telling us through the wind who you are?" There was another EMF hit as the K2's lights brightly flashed. Unknown at the time, an EVP was recorded that said, "My name is Lou."

I asked whatever spirit energies may be near to come closer. Another gust of wind rustled the clinging branch leaves as it made its way toward us.

The K2 meter begins to respond when an EVP was recorded.

"Kat?" I turned to see Leslie Minth sitting at the opposite end of the short wall. She looked toward me, "I'm getting pressure on the top of my head. Almost like a shot in the head type thing. Just real pressure... all in the front." She held her hand up in front of her face.

Leslie, a sensitive, is often able to pick up or sense spirits. At that particular moment she had the sensation that a spirit was near and had incurred a head trauma. I nodded and decided to change my line of questions.

"Were you shot in the war? Were you killed in the war on Mackinac Island. Please let us know by lighting the lights up." Nothing. EMF levels were flat.

I continued asking questions, allowing time after each for a response. "Were you killed in a fight... a fight of some kind?"

"Were you shot? Did you get injured in the head?" It was just after the last question that I thought I'd heard a responding voice. I repeated, "Did you get injured in the head?" We all listened as another strong gust of wind shook the trees, but EMF levels remained stubbornly flat.

Investigators look on as K2 meter continues to respond.
Leslie Minth (2nd from left) felt the spirit had sustained
an injury to his head. She may well have been right.

Upon later review, we would discover I had been right. After asking about a head injury, a voice was recorded. A very quiet male voice, "I did." Moments after that disembodied voice, my audio recorder, still lying by the tombstone where I had first knelt, picked up a second EVP, "I still have a bump on my head."

That seemed to be the last of it. Whatever spirit energy had been around was either gone or simply uncommunicative. It was time to move on to the next investigation, but there was time for one last question.

"If you do want us to leave, we will do that. Please light up all those lights again." I said, referring to the K2 meter the investigator to my right held. "If you do, we will leave."

The K2 came alive, flashing all five lights just as my video camera cut off, the last of it's charge drained. It signaled an end to this session.

I met up with Bev and took a moment to tell her about our session. I asked how it had gone for her. She shrugged, looked around and said, "Pretty dead for us." She gave me one of those smiles, "pun intended" and walked away. Yes, that would be my sister.

So, the few pieces of recorded evidence indicated someone with the name of Lou, possibly a soldier, sustained a head injury that resulted in his death. We took what little we had and began historical research that took us way back in time.

His name was Lewis Howard. Howard arrived at the fort in 1808 as Captain of Artillery and would later take the role of Post Commander. In January 1811, Commander Howard was involved in a tragic sleigh riding accident, an accident in which he sustained a severe head trauma. Lewis Howard died from his injuries.

Several historical records indicate the commander's body is buried at Post Cemetery. Exactly where is unknown. It may, in fact, have been Captain Howard's body lying beneath the "Unknown Soldier" tombstone I knelt before.

Was it the spirit of Lewis (Lew) Howard communicating with us from beyond the grave? Were the head injury Leslie sensed and the resulting EVPs related to injuries Howard sustained in the sleigh accident?

Story Eleven:
The Death Trail

Assisted by: Todd Clements, Haunts of Mackinac

Password: sfskt

HE IS KNOWN AS HARVEY, one of the ghosts said to haunt Mission Point Resort. Harvey is not his real name; rather, it is the name given to him by Todd Clements in sensitivity to his living relatives.

Harvey was a college student on the island when the building that is now Mission Point Resort was Mackinac College. As Todd tells us, Harvey had fallen deeply in love with a young lady. Unfortunately, she broke up with him leaving Harvey destitute.

It was February, the dead of winter. A deep freeze had settled over the island. Long nights and short days did little to improve Harvey's disposition. One day, unable to cope with the loss of his lady-love, Harvey wandered from the warmth of Mackinac College to a back road on Mackinac Island. Finding a spot, he sat down under a tree, propped up a shotgun and ended his life.

When Harvey did not return to the college, search teams went out but he was not found. His body remained undiscovered until that summer, months after his actual death.

Harvey's death was recorded as a suicide. Todd, however, wonders if it may have been murder. There were some facts behind Harvey's death that are curious.

In his research, Todd contacted a state police officer. The officer had apparently spoken to local authorities on the case and gained some insight into the details. According to the state police officer, there remained some interesting, unanswered questions.

The first was the death weapon. It was never found. When police arrived at the scene, no guns of any sort were near the body. The second was that Harvey had sustained two shots to the head. Based on descriptions found in police reports of the death scene and autopsy, the officer told Todd he thought it was likely a shotgun.

How can someone shoot themselves twice, in the head, with a shotgun? Well, it's actually possible. There is at least one report of a shotgun suicide where the victim used several rounds to finalize the act. Todd, however, believes the angle of the shot makes Harvey's suicide questionable.

Was it suicide or murder? We hoped to find out while investigating the area where Harvey's remains were found.

Unfortunately, it was at this point in our daytime investigations when Bev had to return to Mission Point Resort to take care of business. That left Todd and I to continue.

We cut across a narrow trail past the remains of an old quarry embankment. Although the forest had nearly hidden it away, there were still areas of the embankment where hard-edged stone was exposed. Their sharp angles were clear reminders of the hard work and long hours nineteenth century soldiers put in as they gathered stone to build Fort Mackinac.

Gathering fort stone was not an easy task. The workers would burn fires for hours over the overhanging rocks then pour cool water on the red hot sections. The cool water would explode the rock.

As we moved farther into the wooded trail, the sound of carriages and tourist chatter faded. We came to a part of the island where few visitors go. Though Todd didn't know the exact location where Harvey's body was found, he knew it began in this general area, the Y intersection of Bicycle Road and Quarry Trail.

Kat gives final direction prior to commencement of teams investigations.

It was a little after 2:00 p.m. The sun was just beginning to drift toward its westward plunge. Fingers of warm rays filtered through the trees shedding faint light on our gathered group. To be very honest, we had no idea where this investigation would take us. Almost anything was possible, and that made it an exciting part of this great island adventure.

The group broke into teams. Approximately fifteen joined me on a narrow trail headed north while another group followed Todd east.

This investigation would last approximately thirty minutes— not a long time but long enough to capture evidence. We headed off down a dirt trail leading deeper into the woods. A few dozen yards in, we stopped. The group separated slightly but remained close enough to maintain visual contact. Silence settled around with only the distant sound of birds breaking the quiet. Once we adjusted to the natural sounds, an EVP session began.

I called out to the student, using his actual name (not the fictitious name of *Harvey*). "Come to us. We're not here to harm you. We want to find out what happened. My name is Kathleen. Some call me Kat."

After a pause I continued, allowing enough time between each question for a response. "Come to us. We're just trying to understand what happened to you. Did you shoot yourself? Did you commit suicide?"

It was then, surrounded by dense woods and shrubbery, the K2's lights started to flash and, at the same time, the Mel-Meter EMF readings spiked. I called to the group making sure they had their cell phones turned off. Investigators have to be very careful with electronic devices like cell phones, walkie-talkies, and remote controls. Their incoming signals will quickly set off most types of EMF meters. In this instance, however, all phones remained off.

Thinking we may have picked up on Harvey, we directed questions to him. Questions continued, each related to events surrounding the student's death. Everything remained quiet, calm. Without continued EMF fluctuations, I mentally dismissed the earlier EMF reaction. It could be a natural occurrence. There are naturally flowing waves of energy that move through our atmosphere. They are often caused by unseen power grids, radio waves, or even naturally occurring earth energy.

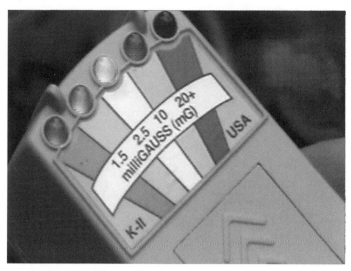

The K2 meter goes off as an EVP is recorded

However, things changed when our line of questions moved to the presence of a young, beautiful woman.

"Was she beautiful?" I asked. "Was she young and beautiful? Is that why you liked her so much?" The K2 lights flickered rapidly, seeming to respond to each question.

I asked if we were talking to a man? The K2 again responded. I asked if the man with us was Harvey (using the student's real name). No response. Then I asked if it was someone besides the college student. With that, the K2's lights rapidly flashed full red. If the K2 was actually signaling a spirit's presence, it was not the spirit of Harvey.

Although we don't consider EMF spikes alone as evidence of a paranormal event, the consistency suggested we might capture something on the audio to validate the responses. As it would turn out, we did.

I had asked if the female was beautiful. The captured response was, "Yes."

Perhaps one of our most intriguing audio clips was spoken in French. There were two distinct voices. The first was a higher pitched voice, perhaps a woman or child, and the second was clearly a man.

The young woman or child's voice said, "Boujou," which is French for "Hello." The man's response was much quieter but the first words sounded quite a bit like the name "Josephine" spoken with a strong French accent.

For a brief moment, the man's quiet words were muffled by our talking, and only the last portion of the sentence heard. Not understanding French, we needed help with the translation. We turned to our friend, Brad Blair.

Brad is a key member of the respected paranormal team, Upper Peninsula Paranormal Research Society. Fortunately, Brad is conversant in both traditional French and its French-Canadian dialect. He was more than happy to attempt a translation.

He quickly confirmed the first word, "Boujou" (hello). According to Brad, that was rather clear, but the responding male voice was much quieter. He would need a day or two for closer analysis.

In a few days he came back and shared his conclusion. The words were French-Canadian, and the male's response was not the name Josephine but rather the phrase, "Je m'accabl." Brad provided his translation, "I am overwhelmed."

It was a sliver of conversation, perhaps a fleeting energy that moved past us on the trail that warm fall afternoon. That, like so much of the island's history, remains unknown.

Before we concluded this story and just a few weeks before we sent it off to our publisher, something interesting happened. Completely by accident, we met a man who had been a tour guide and carriage driver for the Mackinac Island Carriage Tour Company the summer Harvey's body was discovered. He was not only an employee of the carriage company but also one of the first men to discover Harvey's body that hot summer's day. His name is Charley.

The summer of 1969, Charley was a young man of around twenty. As he recalled, the body was discovered during or shortly after the Chicago to Mackinac Yacht Races.

That warm July morning, Charley led the first carriage tour of the day. As part of the regular tour, he stopped at Arch Rock to rest the horses and allow the guests to stretch their legs and take photographs.

Waiting for his guests to return, Charley stood talking to the man at the rest stop who was assigned to help with the horses and carriage during break time. They were chatting when two little island boys on bicycles came out of the woods. They told the men they had just found a "drunk yahtzee" in the woods. The word "yahtzee" is island slang referring to the people associated with the yacht races.

Charley wondered why a yahtzee would wander off this far from the downtown district and decided to check it out. He asked the boys to take him there.

According to Charley, they wandered south in the woods maybe 100 yards. That's when he smelled a thick, cloyingly sweet, pungent odor. It was the kind of scent that coats the back of the throat causing an involuntary gag reflex. Charley stopped, instinctively knowing what lay beyond the trees and shrubs was not a drunk yahtzee.

He moved closer and what he feared was instantly confirmed. The body was propped up against a tree in a sitting position and wore a red and black hunting jacket. His remains were a ghastly, unforgettable sight and one Charley preferred not to describe in detail.

As Charley continued to explain, it was a not a shotgun but a Winchester 33 rife that the student used. Charley also remembers a note pinned to the young man's jacket that said he was "going back to his planet" because he "couldn't stand it here anymore."

Was it an actual suicide note or one placed on Harvey to fake a suicide? That is unknown; although according to Charley, everyone in town believed, without question, it was suicide.

We asked Charley if there had been any talk of Harvey's girlfriend. He responded there hadn't been. People in town thought the young guy had "weirded out."

"Do you think he was high?" I asked, considering the rising drug culture of the late 1960s, especially among college-age students.

Charley didn't think so. As he explained, the island in the

winter is a very confining place. There isn't much to do and the harsh winter months took an emotional toll on many of the Mackinac College students. Charley hesitated a moment before continuing. "Then, of course, there was the MRA."

The Moral Re-Armament group was a multi-national moral and spiritual movement with a philosophy and ferocity that some believed had the characteristics of a cult. The MRA had a strong presence and a huge influence on Mackinac College. We will share more on the MRA in our investigation of Mission Point Resort.

Before we conclude this story, we have to share one very curious thing discovered after our investigation. Almost all of the video after the Post Cemetery investigation was blank.

I would like to say the cause was battery failure. Perhaps the fresh battery I put in after the cemetery investigation had a charge problem. However, the camera showed the battery fully charged, and the tape I had used, fresh from its packaging, had run to the end.

Adding to the bizarreness, when I fast forwarded through the videotape I discovered, about twenty minutes into it, something had recorded. It was the last portion of our investigation on Harvey's Death Trail. The recorded segment ran perhaps a minute or two and then cut off. How strange.

The piece recorded occurred after we had moved into a deeper, more remote section of the trail, a dozen yards or more from the site where our earlier EVPs were captured. Dawn James, an investigator and sensitive who has worked with us in the past, felt a pulling energy in one section on the path. The trees and shrubs hugged close to the trail's edge. We settled in and started a session.

The recorded video kicked in just after I asked if anyone had been killed on the trail. The K2 meter, held by Dawn, went full red.

I asked, "Is this a place where someone was murdered?" The meter's lights continued to rapidly flash. If this was a spirit response, its energy was close, strong, and agitated. Very agitated.

"OK. OK. Step away now. Back off. Slow down. I know you're excited about something. We're here." With that, the K2 lights went dark.

A still image of the only video recorded on Harvey's Death Trail.

I asked if the energy was a man. When no response came, I asked if it was a woman. Still no response. A member of the group glanced at me, saying they thought it was a child's spirit.

"Is this a child?" I questioned. To that the meter responded, lights flashed quickly then dimmed. It was not long after this, the video cut out.

Although video was lost for the remainder of the afternoon, audio recorders did capture some very interesting EVPs during this session.

We asked if a person had died on this trail. The EVP said, "Help me hang 'em."

Further K2 responses indicated three or more spirit energies with us: a man, a woman, and a child. There had been a fight on the trail, and a woman and man were killed.

When asked if someone had been shot, an EVP said, "no one."

This leads us to believe there was a physical confrontation somewhere in the area involving three or more people. A man and woman died, though not from gunfire, and one of them may have been hung. What had become of the child?

Although we did not make a connection to Harvey, we did leave this afternoon session certain there was a spirit connection made. It was another island tragedy of unknown time or cause. What had happened on this trail? With centuries of unrecorded history on the island, the answer may never be known.

I should conclude by saying I've used the same video camera on many investigations since then with no further problems. I've even reused the videotape. It recorded fine. What caused the video problem is unknown. The sole video clip recorded that afternoon can be found in our Secret Room.

Our search for Harvey's spirit continues. Based on the description of the location Charley gave us, we think we have a good idea where the college student's remains were found. We'll head there for our next haunted weekend on Mackinac Island. Perhaps then Harvey's spirit will answer the questions surrounding the mystery of his death, and the truth will finally be known.

Story Twelve:
Rifle Range Trail

Mackinac Island, Michigan
Assisted by: Todd Clements, Haunts of Mackinac

Password: sfwc330

THE LAST STOP ON OUR daytime investigation was Rifle Range Trail. The trail is said to have served as a shooting range for soldiers back in the time Fort Mackinac was an active military base.

People walking through this trail have heard the sound of musket fire, had their hair and clothing pulled, and had rocks thrown at them from the surrounding woods. The fleeting apparition of a soldier dressed in full military attire has also been reported wandering the trail and surrounding woodlands.

Some believe this may be the spirit of Private James Brown. Private Brown was a soldier at Fort Mackinac who, in 1828, shot and killed Corporal Hugh Flynn in the fort's mess hall. He was tried, convicted, and executed. Up to the moment of his death Private Brown swore his innocence, claiming it was not intentional murder but an accident. It was especially noteworthy because it is the only known hanging on Mackinac Island.

There was much controversy associated with Brown's sentence. In January 1830, just a month before his execution, a petition was passed around the island and signatures collected requesting an end to his death sentence. It was submitted to President Jackson but was denied. Private James Brown was hung February 1, 1830.

Todd shares the history of paranormal activity along the trail.

Todd believes a portable gallows was set up on Rifle Range Trail and Brown executed here. Is Private James Brown the ghostly apparition seen on this trail?

There is yet another fleeting spectral image roaming the area. A vision that only a rare few have seen. It is the figure of something that appears half man, half reptile. Several describe the creature's head similar to a turtle.

Todd claims to have seen it once. The image was clear enough for him to describe. It had the body of a man dressed in Native American clothing and the head, to Todd's eyes, looked very much like a turtle. It was one of his more unsettling island experiences.

Todd, uncertain what reference to use for this vision, said, "...it appeared to be a Native American demon."

Many believe that half-human/half-creature beings are signs of a demon, but could there be another explanation?

Our research led us to America's far southwest and its early civilizations: the Pueblo, Hopi, and Navajo tribes. Each held strong traditions and beliefs in supernatural beings called Kachinas. Mostly benevolent, these beings lived among the early peoples teaching them basic living skills and how to live in harmony with nature. There are many Kachinas, each representing the spirit of earth, whether it is a bird, plant, or animal. A reptile was one of the earth spirit Kachinas.

During sacred ceremonies, Native Americans would wear a headdress resembling a chosen earth spirit, their totem. They believed by wearing a headdress taken from these creatures (feathers, skins, horns, or heads) the wisdom and/or strength of the animal would flow into their body. If actual pieces of the animal could not be worn, they would create headdresses resembling the image.

The turtle was a desired totem and thought to possess strong powers. It represented longevity, endurance, survival skills, and patience. Although slow in movement, it survives by the strength of its outer shell. The turtle holds earth's energies and all of earth's mystical powers.

This brings us back to Mackinac Island's earlier name, Michilimackinac, the *large mud turtle*. Might this rare vision seen on Rifle Range Trail be the spirit of an early warrior wearing his totem headdress, the turtle; or could it be the very spirit for which the island was named? Michilimackinac Kachina... *the turtle* island spirit.

Bev and I have never seen this half-man/half-reptile vision on the trail, so we cannot attest to its truth. However, what we can tell you from past investigations is that there are some crazy EMF fluctuations found in this area. Some may last a second or two, others a minute or more.

Because of their unpredictable nature and the fact that we have never captured an EVP or any recordable evidence on the trail, we dismissed these EMF spikes as likely coming from stray radio signals. We discovered a few radio towers around the island. Although none of the towers are near Rifle Range Trail, the hits could be associated with floating radio signals or shortwave radio transmissions.

One of the electrical engineers we spoke with told us that heavily wooded areas should block out most, if not all, of these errant signals. On Rifle Range Trail, however, there is a wide path cut out with the town clearly visible beneath. The likelihood of this wide path allowing radio waves to filter through is very possible.

So, as mentioned, we have dismissed these unpredictable EMF spikes as not paranormal. Until, that is, our last investigation.

We were conducting an EVP session around mid-point on the old trail. It was shortly after 3:00 p.m. when a member of our group, called to me. She was pointing toward the top of the hill.

"I just saw something up there," she said.

"What?" I asked, my eyes scanning the area.

"A shadow figure. Dark. It was standing at the top there looking down at us, then disappeared into the woods."

"What did it look like?"

"I don't know. Just this dark figure."

The group looked around, searching. If something had been there, it was gone.

Ridge at trailhead where member of team reported seeing a shadow person

I resumed the EVP session, again attempting my broken Ojibwa. There continued to be a few frustrating, inconsistent EMF fluctuations as we have come to expect in this section of land. We stopped our questions and just stood for some time. Listening. Watching. Only the harsh cry of a nearby crow was heard, his screech almost threatening in its intensity.

Then, what happened on Fort Holmes a few hours before occurred on this trail. A wave of energy swept through the group. Mel-Meters and K2s alike were going off, each validating the other and signaling a moving energy field. The meters stilled as the one lying on the ground a few feet from me went off.

The K2 came to life as questions were asked surrounding a child's presence. I encouraged the child to come close. "Do you feel okay?" That's when our first EVP was recorded. It was quiet—very quiet—the voice of a young boy, "yes."

It was our first piece of recorded evidence on Rifle Range Trail. EMF levels did continue to rise in consistent response to questions regarding the child's parents. Based on those responses, it seemed the child was looking for his mother and father.

Although no EVPs were recorded to support the K2 responses, it was curious and made me recall something Todd had told us a while back. One of the spirits at Mission Point Theater was believed to be that of a young boy looking for his parents.

Looking back, my mind focused on our investigation on Harvey's Death Trail and a possible tragedy that had occurred on that trail. Three people, a man, woman, and child, had been identified. There had been a fight and the man and woman were killed. I wondered what had become of the child?

Was this who were we connecting with now? Is it possible that poor lost child, searching for his parents, had attached itself to one of us? Unfortunately, if it was a child's energy it was fleeting. The K2s dimmed and things quieted again.

As paranormal investigators, we learn to expect the unexpected. Even then, there are times when something happens that takes us by complete surprise. What happened next, I have to admit, was one of those off-guard moments.

It was 3:30 p.m. We had wrapped our session on Rife Range Trail and were heading back to Mission Point Resort. There would be a few hours' break for the group allowing them time to rest or head into town before the nighttime ghost tours and investigations began.

Our group was nearing the lower third of Rife Range Trail. I was explaining to everyone these investigations and the evidence collected would be in our next book and on our website. That's when the lights of the K2 meter started flashing. All five lights, indicating a strong energy was near.

Liz Ammerman and her daughter Alyssa were the first to notice. They watched in surprise as the lights continued to flash. "When you started talking about your book it started going off." Liz said, a question in her eyes.

The team gathers as the K2 meter begins to respond to Kat's questions.

I scratched my head and watched as the K2 lights continued to flash then slowly dimmed. Was it just another floating radio wave or stray energy field? I could not imagine why any spirit energy would respond to the mention of our book. Then a thought came to mind. It was a rather far out, obscure possibility, but why not give it a try? In the paranormal field—yet to be fully understood—can anything be too obscure?

With all the investigations Bev and I have been on and all the stories we've written, I wondered if one of the spirits had attached itself to me?

I asked, "Are you someone from one of the stories in our book?" The K2 hit. "Is it someone attached to me after all the investigations." The K2 meter went crazy. I went through a few names, with slight responses from the K2. It wasn't until I mentioned David Whitney's name that the K2 blasted full red and the Mel-Meter shot up several points. With that spike, an EVP was recorded. It said, "Call me David."

I was completely taken aback. The story of David Whitney Jr. and his family was in our first book and part of our investigation of the beautiful Whitney Restaurant in Detroit. David Whitney Jr., during the turn-of-the-century, was Detroit's wealthiest lumber baron. For our story on the Whitney Restaurant, we completed months of research on David and his family. In fact, it was one of those stories and families that get under your skin. After a time, it was as if I had gotten to know them personally. They were a very close family.

Members of the group gathered around me as I called out other members of the Whitney family. The next EMF spike came with mention of David's daughter, Flora.

What? Of all people, Flora Whitney!

Flora was the Whitney family *wild child*. She married a man against her father's wishes. In fact, Mr. Whitney was so opposed to the wedding he threatened to disinherit her if she went through with it. Well, despite her father's threats, she did marry the man. Her father relented at the end but never approved of the union. It seemed Mr. Whitney's concerns were valid. Flora's husband ended up breaking her heart. The marriage ended in a divorce, which was quite scandalous for its time.

At the mention of divorce and Flora, the EMF again shot up. It seemed Flora had indeed arrived here, at this most unlikely place. I laughed, completely taken aback. "Flora, what are you doing attached to me? Geesh, get away!" With that statement, EMF levels immediately dropped. Both Mr. Whitney and Flora were gone. I shook my head. That was pretty crazy.

It was not, however, the end. A moment later the K2 and Mel-Meters around me again went off again. Something new had arrived. The others looked at me as I shrugged. What in the world was going on here?

It seemed another spirit from my past was with me, someone from our second book. The K2 responded full red when I asked if it as a man involved with a murder.

Dawn James, a friend and fellow investigator, noticed when I had mentioned the name Crouch her K2 immediately responded. She asked me go back to that. I did.

"Is this a member of the Crouch family?" EMF levels immediately rose and, we later discovered another EVP was recorded. A male voice that simply said, "Correct."

The Crouch murders, one of Michigan's greatest unsolved murders was a story in our second book. Jacob Crouch, wealthy businessman and family patriarch, along with members of his family and a visiting friend were all murdered in their beds during a violent thunderstorm in late November 1883. Although there were several suspects, including members of their own family, the murderer or murderers were never identified. To this day it remains unsolved.

The Crouch story was a strange one indeed and one that took months to complete. The facts behind the case and the bizarre people involved were compelling. I almost become obsessed with the research. By the end of that project, I felt as though I knew each strange person associated with the family. EMFs elevated with mention of the murder and the fact that more than one person was involved. Unfortunately, no EVPs were recorded that would provide further information. The energy that had come to visit was quickly gone.

EMF levels remained flat for a few long seconds only to come back stronger than ever. I could feel the building pressure in my head as the swirl of energy moved through the group and around me setting off K2 and Mel-Meters. Oh God, who had come through now?

I shook my head to clear it and glanced at my watch. It was nearing 4:00 p.m. We were way past our scheduled end time and had to leave. As soon as I said that, EMF levels dropped. Whoever the next spectral visitor was decided to leave.

As we made our way back to the town, I remained quiet. Anyone who knows me knows that is very rare! I felt emotionally and physically drained, not because of the several miles we had walked that afternoon but, rather, from what had just happened.

My mind was whirling. It was as if a vortex opened and spirit energies from our past investigations came through. Was that the mystery of Rifle Range Trail? Did these electromagnetic fields that constantly rush through the trail, whatever their origin, collide from time to time creating a vortex?

For those unfamiliar with a vortex, it is an area of high energy concentration that may come from natural magnetic earth energy, spiritual, or other unknown sources. A vortex is often considered to be a gateway or portal to other realms, both spiritual and dimensional.

Sunspots and sun flares will influence a vortex. Sunspots are a powerful source of rotating energy. From time to time their undulating power explodes from the sun's surface causing flares. These flares, filled with billions of charged radioactive particles are thrown out into the universe, often reaching the earth's own magnetic field. Flares, especially the larger ones, can affect many aspects of the earth and its atmosphere.

What Bev and I discovered is that on September 27, 2012, a huge sun flare occurred. Its size and scope were so powerful astronomers were a bit nervous. They watched and waited to see what type of impact the flare would have on Earth. They hoped enough of this powerful divergence of solar, radioactive particles would sufficiently be deflected by the earth's magnetic field to minimize affects.

This massive sun flare reached Earth around mid-day September 29. The very day, the very time, we were on Rifle Range Trail.

Could this be an explanation for the bizarre events that happened on the trail that warm Saturday afternoon? The already charged atmosphere on the trail collided with the charged particles from the sun flare creating some form of crazy super-vortex?

Even without the impact of the flare, perhaps the naturally charged region of Rifle Range Trail can, on its own, produce vortexes—openings to the other side. Is it through these portal dimensions the soldier, shadow people, and Native American Turtle Man come?

There is so much we don't understand. That's the frustrating part about paranormal research, but that's also the exciting part. It's what drives most of us forward.

Introduction:
Mission Point Resort

6633 Main St
Mackinac Island, MI 49757
906-847-3312

WAITING WITH EXCITEMENT, LIKE ALWAYS, Kat and I stood in line for the Ferry to Mackinac Island. Leaving the car behind we would take a step back in time to the 1800s. Once on board we sat back and again marveled at the Mackinaw Bridge, an engineering wonder. The ferry moved quickly, breaking the water, creating a large wake. Turning our attention east, looking through the water's spray, we saw a small green island that quickly grew. Standing on a bluff facing us was the unforgettable Grand Hotel, a welcoming beacon.

On this trip, however, we were headed to the east side of the island, Mission Point Resort. It was a beautiful site as our horse-drive carriage approached. Deep green lawn cascaded down the front of the hotel, its lawn dotted with white chairs for guests. Seagulls seem to float overhead landing in the dark blue Lake Huron waters. The drive way was overflowing with a colorful array of flowers taking us to the main lobby.

Upon entering, the lobby's distinctive ceiling immediately captured our attention. Eighteen enormous beams reached to meet in the center, its design specifically constructed to represent a teepee, a symbol to this land's Native American heritage.

We were here for another one of our ghost hunter's weekends at the resort. These weekends are always exciting. Each day there are tours provided by Todd Clements and his Haunts of Mackinac tour guides. Kat and I take guests on Saturday afternoon investigations to some of the more paranormally active spots on the island, with the help of Todd Clements of course.

Today, Mission Point Resort and Mackinac Island are bustling with activity. Guests move in and out of historic shops. Horse-drawn carriages take people across town. It's hard to imagine what Mission Point was like nearly two hundred years ago.

In the beginning, before written language, Native American's claimed the island was sacred. The most holy part of the island was the southeastern corner. It was the special home for the Great Manitou. Every spring he rises from the bottom of Lake Huron to return. Yes, it is a special and sacred place for the spirits.

In 1823, Mackinac Island consisted of Fort Mackinac and a fur trading post, but that doesn't mean no one was there. It was a hub of activity for the military, fur traders, and Indians. That's about the time a young, zealous Presbyterian missionary, Reverend William Ferry, stepped onto the island. His job was to teach the Indians. Reverend Ferry would build a school and church by the fort.

What better place to teach and pray with his congregation than the island's most sacred spot, the southeast corner of land. His first task was the school, which he named Mission House. It opened in 1825 and consisted of 112 students of Indian, white, and metis (mixed blood) heritage. Most of the children lived at school where they were taught the English culture, language, and Christian religion.

Mission Point Church is one of the oldest in the Midwest.

About five years later, Mission Point Church was erected, one of the first protestant churches in the Midwest. Walking from town toward Mission Point Resort, the church is visible on the right side, close to the water, just before entering the main resort grounds. It is open to visitors today and is considered one of many historic sites on the island.

Reverend Ferry is given credit for naming that part of the island Mission Point because of the church and school. Unfortunately, the good reverend lost his calling. Possibly the winters were just too brutal for his young family. Whatever the reason, he left Mission House in the mid-1830s and moved to Grand Rapids. He left the ministry and ended up making his fortune in lumber and politics.

The school remained empty until the late 1840s. Then Edward and Mary Frank bought the property. Originally from New York, the couple would end up raising their children there. Over the next few years, they added a third story to the school and turned it into the Mission Hotel. For over ninety years the family ran the Mission Hotel. They were committed and loved the island.

Historic plaque tells the history of Mission House

Initially the hotel was used by fur traders and people moving back and forth across the straits. The rooms were pretty Spartan but good enough. Edward and Mary were used to hardship and hard work. The island was a challenge that they embraced, and the hotel served its purpose of clean shelter for guests.

Over the years, many famous people stayed at Mission Hotel as the island began to blossom into a tourist attraction. Edward Everett Hale wrote "Man Without A Country" while at Mission Hotel. He loved the deep blue waters of Lake Huron and found watching and listening to the waves cascade on the shore inspirational.

Near the turn of the century, Mackinac slowly merged into one of the country's favorite vacation spots. The Frank family did very well, but there was a growing problem they would soon discover. The hotel was very simple, almost rustic, and guests were becoming accustomed to better accommodations on the island. Finally, the Great Depression of the late 1920s and 1930s hit. It was more than the family could financially handle. They left the hotel and moved on to other ventures. Once more the hotel was abandon and remained so until 1940.

Edward, his wife, and at least one of their children were buried on Mackinac according to a family blog site. The Franks worked hard at Mission Hotel, pouring their hearts and souls into it for decades. Possibly, Edward and Mary remain along with their children or the many guests that stayed. In the paranormal community, people often lean towards the notion that spirits stay because of strong emotional attachments. Is that what happened here?

Today Mission House is maintained by the Island State Park and is the summer residence for many island workers. Unfortunately, the house is closed to visitors.

During the rise of communism, a new social consciousness began to form: a global, multi-national movement, more a state of mind than a religion. The Oxford Group, later called Moral Re-Armament (MRA) was a way of life filled with love, purity, and unselfishness. The charismatic Dr. Frank Buchman led the MRA in its evangelistic campaign around the globe. Many world leaders believed in his principles and believed in him. There was strong support in the USA from some very famous people including Harry Truman and Henry Ford, just to name a few.

The passionate Buchman quickly grew his followers as the Nazi movement escalated. He believed a war was about to start in the mid-1930s and started his crusade for peace. Buchman even went so far as to travel to Germany attempting to mediate with Hitler. According to most reports, the two men never did meet.

One spring afternoon, in 1942, he just happened to be staying with Henry Ford and his wife Clara. Buchman mentioned the MRA had not yet decided on a place for the summer convention. Mrs. Ford was more than willing to offer a suggestion. With an enthusiasm Buchman found irresistible, she recommended Mackinac Island.

More irresistible was the price. Clara did some fast-talking with the governor of Michigan, and the MRA could rent the land and large hotel for $1 per year. By the 1950s it would become their world headquarters. They stayed there until the mid-sixties.

The first thing Buchman did was build a state-of-the-art theater, which opened in 1955. Why wouldn't he want a state-of-the-art theater? After all the MRA had more than twenty different casts performing in plays and musicals around the world. Naturally the world headquarters needed the best theater possible. Many called it "the theater of hope."

We can only imagine the emotional speeches, plays, and musical entertainment that went on promoting a joyful life. Famous directors, actors, and choreographers were involved in many productions. Themes focused not on the actual world but, rather, the world and people as they should be. Mackinac was known around the world for its theatrical performances.

The adjacent building is the sound stage. The main sound stage is expansive—80x120 foot. When completed, it was the second largest in the country. Many movies and TV shows were produced in the sound stage.

Buchman received encouragement and aid from scores of Hollywood celebrities, directors, and producers such as Alfred

Hitchcock and Cecil B. DeMille. Remarkably, more than 250 volunteer workers from all over the world helped to construct these impressive buildings.

After construction of the theater, the MRA erected the main lodge, a remarkable piece of architecture. As mentioned before, Kat and I were awed the first time we saw the lodge. According to Mission Point Resort's website, it is one of the most distinctive architectural structures on the island. Nine-ton majestic trusses converge at a height of thirty-six feet. Just as its designers intended, it resembled a magnificent sixteen-sided teepee.

Tepee design symbolic of ancient Indian prophecy foretelling of peace

Just building the main lodge was a remarkable task. The large trusses were brought from Bois Blanc Island during the summer. More than 3000 tons of supplies were stockpiled. Islanders worked all winter but by March were out of supplies. The lake was frozen and the barge could not get through to deliver the needed lumber. Buchman and the crews were beside themselves. The work had to be done before the convention. Now what?

Then came the *March Miracle*. A warm wind blew the ice from the main channel and workers cut a patch of frozen water from the shore. The barge was able to push through the ice and deliver the supplies.

Buchman built the tepee-domed lodge for a very symbolic reason. This structure fulfills the Indian prophecy found on the Mission Point Resort Website. "Someday, on the east end of the island, a great teepee will be erected. All nations will come there and learn about peace." That statement is really what the MRA movement was all about.

Frank Buchman was without question a charismatic and inspirational figure who led the global organization until his death in 1961. He started groups such as Alcoholics Anonymous. The uplifting, enthusiastic singing group Up With People started on Mackinac Island and would become a worldwide phenomenon. Of course, he was a good man. There is no question he was a good man.

Or was he? Not everyone loved Buchman, neither his leaders or the MRA. Many were completely opposed to the group. They didn't trust the fervent commitment required by its followers. Some thought he might be a supporter of Hitler. After all, one of his close friends, Henry Ford, believed in Hitler's movement.

Charley, a man who lived and worked on the island for a number of years, spoke to Kat and me about his time there. He clearly remembers the MRA and thought it was a cult, into mind control just like Hitler. He believed Buchman supported fascism and his followers were strange and different. This was a common view held by many island residents and numerous groups. People either loved the MRA, were suspicious, or avoided them.

When the MRA moved their headquarters to Switzerland, the complex was given to Mackinac College. It only operated from 1966 to 1970. Unfortunately, the winters were just too harsh to attract enough students. The island is brutal and unforgiving at that time of year and is pretty much cut off from the mainland. This isolated form of existence just didn't fit with the needs of most social college students.

The four years it operated, however, education was built around MRA beliefs. Students who attended were committed and devoted to a higher education and the college. Even today there is an active website for Mackinac College alumni and those interested. Its forward-thinking president, S. Douglas Cornell, was a strong MRA follower who wanted the students to do more than get an education. He wanted a pure learning experience. In a quote taken from one of his speeches on the website (http://www. mintakadesign.com/Mackinac-College/), Dr. Cornell stated the students must:

> *"...learn the difference between knowledge and wisdom. (Students) will have the chance to seek the wisdom that does not always come with knowledge..."*

The college appeared to be very advanced and forward thinking. In spite of that, suspicions persisted, especially by the islanders. They did not like or trust the college being there. Back to Charley, our friend who worked for Mackinac Island Carriage Tours in the late 60s. He remembers being given specific instructions to never say anything bad about the college or students while driving passengers.

Charley recounted the day he broke the rules and was called in to the supervisor's office and given a reprimand. In speaking to us, he swears that at times the MRA would put spies on the carriages. In Charley's opinion, the students stuck to themselves, and Charley, along with many islanders, pretty much stayed away from that group of young people.

Probably one of the most notorious college students was the young man referred to as *Harvey*. As mentioned in our story based on daytime investigations of the island, *Harvey* is not his real name. It is the name we use in deference to his remaining family. He had a girlfriend at the college. Just two young people madly in love—or so Harvey thought. On a blustery winter day, his lady love decided to end their relationship. At least that's the story on the island.

One night Harvey went into the woods. Cut off from his mainland friends and family, he felt alone. Although the weapon was never found, most believe he ended his life with a shotgun. We will never know what drove Harvey to such a horrible state. It is not even known with certainty if it was over a girlfriend. Charley told us that at the time there was no rumor of a girlfriend. Islanders thought the young man just went crazy.

So, was there a breakup? If so, was their breakup more devastating than he could emotionally endure? Maybe it was the frozen wasteland Mackinac turned into during winter or possibly a young man who just lost his way.

Then there are those who talk about Harvey's murder. They question the idea of suicide. Was it a lover's triangle gone wrong? It could be a lot of things. We will never know for sure unless he whispers the truth to someone at the resort or on the trail.

In later years Mission Point turned into the outstanding resort it is today. Yet how much of the past still lives there? How many spirits still call it home? We hope to find answers to a few of these questions during our haunted weekends.

Story Thirteen:
Straights Lodge, Room 2200

Mission Point Resort

Password: har22

DURING OUR HAUNTED WEEKEND ON Mackinac Island events, Kat and I had room 2200 open for investigations. Investigations ran Friday and Saturday until 2:00 AM. Guests signed up for a private time to investigate the room.

Based on the number of teams, the room would be covered most of the day and night. If the room was active, it seemed somewhat certain it would be captured. To ensure full coverage, we left an audio recorder in the room hoping to pick up additional evidence in-between investigations.

Is Harvey still on the island? Some believe the Straits Lodge is where his girlfriend stayed while attending college and that she lived in what is now Room 2200. If that was her actual room, we can only assume Harvey was there visiting his lady love many times.

At Mission Point Resort, Room 2200 is one of several rooms considered to be very active. All sorts of things happen. People hear voices of men, women, and children, shadows have been seen, objects move, and lights or the fan turn on unexpectedly.

During our series of haunted weekend investigations on Mackinac Island and Mission Point Resort, we hoped to one day understand who the spirits are and why they remain. What follows are some of the experiences that occurred during our first two years on Mackinac Island.

Straights Lodge is a short distance from the main lodge. Many of our Haunted Travels guests stay there for our paranormal weekends. That makes it convenient to mingle with friends. Room 2200 is a lovely, cheerful room with a sitting area, TV, and small kitchenette. Overstuffed sofas and chairs rest on a plaid carpet, and the sleeping area contains an abundantly comfortable bed. Numerous windows offer views of the lake and grounds.

It's not known for certain if Harvey's girlfriend actually stayed in this room, but what is certain is many MRA and Mission Point Resort guests have. Over the years it has seen a lot of people.

Some believe the voices and shadows they experience are possibly Harvey. However, there have also been reports of a woman and child heard in the room. What, if anything, would we find?

Generally, Kat and I stay in that room during our Ghost Hunter Weekends—well, sort of. With investigations scheduled until 2:00 am, we don't get to spend a lot of time there.

After listening to the audio we recorded non-stop in the room, we noted many of the guest investigators had questions. We think it's only right that we answer at least a few of those questions now.

Yes, that is our recorder. It is on and we listen to all of it. No, there is no hidden camera in the room. No, we do not feel bad because we received a delicious fruit basket that, by the way, is *ours*. No, there is no liquor in the mini-frigde. Yes, that was a really dumb question to ask the spirits. Yes, we heard you snoring.

Back to the more serious topic of the paranormal. On both weekends the room proved to be highly active, as many guests would find out. Here is a recap of the more bizarre happenings.

Our very first night, Kat and I didn't know what to expect. Going up for a short investigation around 8:00 p.m., we met some people leaving. They were wide-eyed and very excited. Voices had been heard that coincided with their flashlight turning on and off. They were even more excited that they had captured it on video.

For those unfamiliar with the *flashlight method*, it became popular on one of the more well-known reality TV ghost hunting shows. How it works is simple. You slightly unscrew the end of the flashlight until the light goes off. Some in the paranormal believe the spirits, or their energy, are able to respond to questions by turning the light on and off. Kat and I believe the metal is simply heating and cooling, expanding and contracting the flashlight case, turning the light on and off.

We do not use the flashlight method in our investigations. However, if you are a believer, you can see their video in our Secret Room. It does indeed look like the light responded to questions. Whether it's just coincidence or paranormal is your decision.

In any event, activity seemed to be kicking up. Another time Kat and I were in the room with Chris and Rose Peterson. Our session started off rather uneventful until an interesting series of events began.

It started when one of our investigators, Holly Birano, entered the room. The K2 lights suddenly went off. It was almost as if

Holly had brought in or stirred up some kind of energy. After exchanging greeting, she positioned herself along the wall as the investigation continued.

Because of the K2's sudden action, Kat thought she'd see if a spirit had entered and was ready to communicate with us. She asked, "Are you a man?" The K2 lights immediately flashed. She continued, "Are you a woman?" This time the K2 remained dark.

To test the first response, she repeated the question, "Are you a man?" The K2's came to life again, blinking several times. From there she started a series of questions directed at Harvey. Unfortunately, as the questions continued the K2 grew quiet.

It was almost immediately after the K2 quieted Kat felt a breeze. Startled, the five of us looked up surprised to see the ceiling fan on and running at high speed. The closest person to the fan wall switch was Holly. We asked if she might have accidentally brushed up against it. She shook her head saying she had not.

It was then a very soft EVP was captured. It said, "I don't care."

That just didn't seem to relate to anything being asked. The spirit may be residual, re-enacting a conversation from the past. Who it was and what connected the energy here will likely remain a mystery of Room 2200.

Kat continued directing questions towards the young college student, Harvey. No response.

I asked if he turned the fan on because he was hot. No response.

Kat went on, "Was this your room. What's your name?" Nothing. From that point on, it seemed things settled down for the night.

Later, Kat and I returned for another investigation. This time it would just be the two of us. The team that left as we entered was very excited. They'd several experiences including K2 responses and a voice they believed was a child.

We decided to direct our questions to a child. Kat began, "You talked to the last people that were here. Can you talk to us? Can you knock?"

"Can you knock like this," I said and demonstrated by giving two short raps on the table. I paused. Kat and I exchanged glances. There was a response.

"I thought I heard something," Kat said. I had heard it too. Two clear raps. I asked for the response several times and, each time, received a responding rap. This continued for a bit then stopped. If there had been a young child, it had left. Unfortunately, though the raps had been clear, no EVPs were recorded that might help us understand who it may have been or why they remained.

Knocks were heard in the bedroom.

Yet another session was conducted. This time it was three women: Dana, Sasha, and ReNae. They were setting up equipment and getting into position. Over their voices our audio recorder picked up, "I can do it." Do what we don't know. It sounded like a younger man or woman.

The ladies were running their session, each sitting in a different area of the room. One of the women whispered, " I thought I saw a shadow. Did anyone else see it?" Unfortunately, no one had.

Many times in a dark room our eyes play tricks on us and we see things that just aren't there. Yet, what made this interesting is that shortly after the shadow was seen one of their fully charged camera batteries died. Was it a bad battery or a spirit pulling its energy?

Their investigation was coming to an end, and Dana called out, "This is your last chance to let us know you are here." Sasha jokingly said, "This is your last chance."

It was then one of them softly called out. "Hang on, guys, I thought I heard something that said, don't go." She asked if anyone else heard the voice. No one else had, and thinking it was nothing, they left feeling a little disappointed.

What they didn't know is that our recorder had picked up a voice. Though very faint, we believe it said, "Don't go" or "Please go." It was quiet on the recorder but loud enough for one of the investigators to hear the words.

Another weird happening had to do with the room's heater. Our audio recorder picked up several groups talking about how warm the room was. It didn't make much sense, but then, a lot of what happens in Room 2200 doesn't make sense.

One of the groups came in using dowsing rods. Someone mentioned the room was warm. They shrugged it off and continued their session. One individual in the group, Liz Ammerman, held the dowsing rods and commented that the rods were beginning to move. Although the rod movements didn't seem connected to anything in particular, one strange thing did occur. The room's temperature continued to rise.

Halfway through their session an EVP was captured. At the time, there was a lull in the conversation. From out of nowhere, a tortured whisper was recorded. A man's voice said, "Kill me, they won't wake up."

What was that all about? The word "they" implies more than one person. We dug into research but, to our frustration, found nothing to indicate there were ever deaths, fires, or tragedies of any kind at the resort.

The group eventually found the cause for the increasing heat. A thermostat was on a side wall, not easy to reach. Somehow it had been raised all the way to high.

The thermostat was in a location not easily accessible. It was certainly not in a place where a person could lean against it or accidentally bump the knob upward. They wondered how or why the heat was turned up all the way.

Kat and I wondered the same thing. The next day we asked some of the cleaning staff about the thermostat. They told us that it wasn't unusual to find the thermostat had been raised to high, even in the middle of summer. They had no idea how or why it happened.

On other investigations, several groups heard the voice of a young child they thought might be a little girl. Although the voice wasn't recorded, if it was a child, what keeps the young spirit in this room?

During our two years of investigations, multiple groups have claimed to hear a child's voice. We know the Straits Lodge was a college dorm, and a child attachment seems unlikely. Who knows, maybe a young spirit just wanders the grounds. It could be a child from the original Mission House, which sits directly across from the Straits Lodge. It might even be a member of the Frank family or, possibly, the child of a past hotel guest. Our research revealed nothing that would help us understand the presence of a child in this room or, for that matter, the Straits Lodge.

Another session in this room brought Kat and I together with a friend and experienced investigator, Maria Holt-Aistrop. She has a way of attracting spirits. We jokingly tell her it's her natural charm. Once, while the three of us were in the room, Maria brought a toy that had lights and played music. If a child frequented the area, perhaps the toy would draw out the little boy or girl.

When she turned the toy on it sang the alphabet song. What a great way to start an investigation! Maria was talking to any child that might be with us when her fully charged battery died. That frequently happens in this room.

Unfortunately, this time the room remained very quiet. Yes, it seemed our time in the room was pretty much dead, no pun intended. Just a little discouraged, we walked out as a couple entered. They asked us to join them, which we gladly did.

Shortly into the session, Kat spoke, "We understand there is a little child that stays in this room sometime." Briefly pausing, she continued, "Did you hear a voice?"

Maria confirmed she had. When recorders were checked, a voice was heard. It was a younger-sounding voice, possibly a younger male voice. It sounded like the words "together forever."

Could this be our first response from Harvey or, possibly, another young man proclaiming his undying affection for his lady love? Sadly, if those were Harvey's words, his lady love moved on with her life. Harvey can wait and hope, but they will never be together forever.

Maria stated a series of questions asking the spirits what it was like on the other side. "Is it a world of no pain, no sorrow?" Silence followed.

Kat took a turn. "Are you happy, at peace?" With that came a clear response, "No."

The recorded voice was younger. We were stunned to hear that when reviewing audio. I think everyone hopes that most people pass on to a better, happy life. Yet we have a young spirit not at peace. Maybe they want and need to cross over but for some reason just can't. It makes us wonder why some are forced to roam the earth.

What could have happened in this room to cause paranormal activity.

On another occasion Maria was in the room with her daughters, Dana and Sasha, and their friend ReNae. Maria was attempting to find out who was there, and after a few questions asked, "Why do you stay?" The puzzling response, "You're a mother, you should know."

There was also the time Maria was in the room talking to Harvey. This may be the only actual response we have that could be from the young man. Maria asked if he was murdered and, if so, would he give her the name of the person who did it. She ended by saying, "We would like to be able to pass that information on to the police so that justice could be brought for you. Can you tell us who did it?"

The response was, "I don't believe that." Maybe Harvey just doesn't think anyone can help him today. The answer could also support Todd Clements theory that Harvey may have been murdered.

During our weekends there were other EVPs. These are available in our Secret Room.

While reviewing the evidence, Kat and I were a little perplexed about Room 2200. The disembodied voices appeared random. They were from men, women, and even a child. Some seemed to be direct responses to questions. Others were just soft whispers from the dark. The collection of audio evidence appeared to be both intelligent and residual.

Generally, analyzing all recorded evidence, it seemed to Kat and I that the voices seemed lonely or desperate. Such as the heartbreaking EVP, "Kill me, they won't wake up." Or the child's response "No" when asked if he or she was at peace. Another EVP captured the wistful words of a young man, "together forever." What could possibly have happened at this beautiful resort that was so sad and desperate.

Then there were the strange series of events: The time, for example, when Kat and I asked the spirits to knock and we heard responding knocks. When the K2 began to flash and, shortly after, the ceiling fan turned on. The unexplained way the room's thermostat inexplicably turned up. It felt as if someone was playing games with us or trying to get our attention. The whole thing left us scratching our heads.

Connecting history to evidence is very important to us. The voices and what happened in Room 2200 makes it impossible for us to understand. Over the years Straights Lodge has had many guests. For some yet unknown reason, some still remain. We may never know who they are or why they stay.

Most people assume the male voice it the room was Harvey. Maria did get the comment, "I don't believe that" after asking Harvey to tell her who his murderer was so she could tell the police. However, perhaps it was not Harvey but another as yet unidentified spirit.

The activity in this room could also be connected to Edward and Mary Frank or their children. After all, the Franks loved Mackinac and the hotel more than anyone. They dedicated their lives to it and are buried on the island. Maybe they still roam the buildings.

Then there is the Moral Re-Armament and college. For many years reverent groups would gather for different events. I suppose it's possible some of them may stay, in spirit.

Although our research continues, to date we really don't understand why Mission Point Theater and Room 2200 are so active. Without a doubt, the spirits at Mission Point Resort remain a puzzle, and that is why we will go back.

Story Fourteen:
Mission Point Theater

Mission Point Resort

Tours: Todd Clements and Haunts of Mackinac

Password: buck55

A s darkness settled on Mission Point Theater, shifting shadows, voices, and creaks seem to come from everywhere. With the help of Todd Clements and his crew from Haunts of Mackinac, this area would be thoroughly covered on Friday and Saturday nights.

Haunts of Mackinac has led groups through the theater for many years on investigations. They know every dark corner collecting some remarkable evidence. For our weekends they took our guests for theater and soundstage investigations. The ghost hunts are held at night, in the dark, when it's quiet.

The theater and sound stage, when opened in 1955, were state-of-the art for the time period. According to an article in the Mackinaw City Archives written by Frances Roots Hadden, Dr. Frank Buchman received aid and encouragement from scores of Hollywood notables like Alfred Hitchcock and Cecil B. DeMille. To the MRA, good, joyful music and plays were very important. Today, they are both considered paranormally active. Could the spirit and zest of the MRA still exist?

The theater was state of the art when built in the 1950s.

The theater and soundstage are well known for an assortment of activities. This includes shadows and voices. In fact, Todd Clements has a rare photograph of a shadow that was taken in the theater.

It is small and he believes the shadow is a child. It's strange how shadows and voices of children seem to turn up all over the resort.

Here and throughout Mission Point, however, more than voices and shadows have been captured. According to Todd and his tour guides, there are extremely rare doppelganger sightings.

A doppelganger is defined as the exact double of a living person. It is paranormal and many believe it is an evil entity or a trickster. Can you imagine groping your way down the dark theater aisle, unclear vision, only to bump into yourself? Now that would be a chilling experience. Well, on several occasions Todd has been seen at two locations at the same time. Todd moves fast, but not that fast.

We could only hope our weekends would provide evidence of the paranormal. Of course you never know when the spirits will come out.

As it would turn out, however, there would be considerable activity the two weekends we were there. It started off in typical fashion. The group was broken into small teams and given assignments. From there, teams slowly moved through the theater and sound stage.

The theater consists of the main room and balcony. Behind the stage are the dressing rooms. There is also a game room across the main hall.

Though connected together, the sound stage is a separate section. It is basically a large room with several smaller connecting rooms and hallways. You enter through the main hall, which is probably a good twenty feet wide and about eighty feet long. One side is the entrance to the sound stage with a series of windows on the opposite side.

As the investigations progressed, team after team reported to Kat and I. There were a number of strange experiences. At least half a dozen people collected voices on their audio recorders. One woman thought she captured the disembodied voice of a smaller child. Todd claims it happens a lot in the theater and sound stage.

Others reported seeing shadow people. Unfortunately, none were captured on video or still cameras. Since tricks of the eyes are so common in dark or semi-dark environments, unless a shadow person is recorded, these kinds of visions are kept under personal experience category and not considered paranormal evidence.

There were two women who claimed to have been were touched in the theater. When questioned, one lady said she was standing motionless and alone in an aisle. The closest person to her was about six feet away. She was startled when she felt her hair being lightly moved or was gently tugged. There was absolutely nothing and no one near her to cause this. She was just a little shaken while at the same time eager to continue the investigation.

In the theater balcony, our friend Maria Holt-Aistrop, her daughters Dana and Sasha, along with their friend ReNae were getting ready to settle into chairs for a session. Dana sat in a chair next to Maria. Maria, thinking more space between team members would be better, asked her to sit farther away so Dana moved. That's when an EVP was captured that said, "I am so sorry for sitting by you." I was clearly the voice of a gentleman. It seems when Maria talks people listen, living or not.

Though the theater was active for many, Maria and her group would find the most activity in the dressing rooms. These rooms are small, maybe 10x12, with a door at each end. At night, with only a sliver of light coming through the doorways, they are creepy little rooms.

Dressing rooms were very small and dimly lit.

Sitting in the dark, the ladies realized it was hot, very hot. Their thermo gauge registered 78 degrees. That's when Maria decided it was time to take some photos. Snapping off a half dozen shots, she was startled to see a bright white image emerging from the bottom in two pictures. It almost looked like a finger. Could it have been Maria's finger? It's possible, although we have to admit it would have been rather awkward to place your finger in this position as you clicked off shots.

Excitedly the ladies talked about the strange images as Maria continued snapping more photos of the same area. She was attempting to recreate the white glowing object to see if it might be a camera strap, her finger or something else. Her various attempts at trying to find a logical reason came up empty. It remains a mystery.

Paranormal? Or did the photographer's finger
unknowingly move in front of the lens?

Maria then asked the spirit to come close to the gray box, pointing to the K2, and make it light. Almost on cue, the K2 lit and, at the same time, the room suddenly chilled. Checking the temperature, they were surprised to discover the room had dropped from 78 to 64 degrees in just a few seconds. They didn't know what was going on and would later discover some curious disembodied voices were captured.

While they were looking at the photos and trying to recreate the image, a voice from the dark said, "Now she'll know what is going on." Moments later when she was done with the photos another voice added, "Now it's historical here."

Maria believes it is almost as if the spirits were commenting on the photos. "Now she'll know..." when the white image was captured and "it's historical..." after she was done taking pictures.

Finally, as the ladies were getting ready to leave the room, a female voice clearly says, "What are you doing in my room?" If she had her own dressing room, the spirit must have been a diva. Run ladies, divas don't like to share.

Altogether, that dressing room definitely had some sort of paranormal energy. The voices were clearly two separate men and a woman. Who were they? A mystery still to be solved.

One year during our investigation of the sound stage, we were in the hall with two ladies, Holly and Judy. The hall is right outside the stage and approximately twenty by eighty. Todd softly explained that one night he picked up an audio here that said, "He killed me." That is one of several reason why Todd believes Harvey may have been murdered.

Hall outside of the sound stage proved active.

During our time in the hall, not much happened except for a brief five-minute period. Kat was talking to Harvey, "Do you know who your killer was? Who was your killer?"

I followed, "Why did they kill you?" The four of us were stretched along the dimly lit corridor. Faint light from the moon gave everything an almost black and white feel, like an old movie. Holly called out that the K2 just hit yellow.

Suddenly, I saw a light against the inner wall. It was quick, less than a second. I thought my eyes were playing tricks, but Kat saw it too. It seemed like a flashlight. That made sense with all the people investigating. It could easily have been a reflection, but Judy and Holly saw the same quick beam on another wall. We tried to find a reason this happened, what may have caused it, but with no luck.

Just two minutes later Todd came to take us into the stage. At that point a soft but clear child's voice was captured. There is no mistaking the young, soft whisper, "Why did you leave us?" followed by a small singsong, just two notes, "La la." The child sounded like my neighbors' little five-year-old daughter.

Moving toward the stage, Todd mentioned what happened the night before. People saw shadows in the corners and catwalk. Also, one team using a thermal imager picked up a cold, full-bodied figure.

Thermo imagers are a form of camera that measure the temperature of a person or object. Generally people use it in black and white for the clearest picture. Black is cold and white is hot, with varying ranges of gray. When using the camera in color, blue and violet are the coldest colors and yellow or red the warmest.

The four of us entered the sound stage and were instantly swallowed by the darkness. Flashlights on, we moved to different locations in the large room. Once the lights were turned off, I felt alone, totally cut off from everyone. It was impossible to see more than a few feet. We moved to the corners. As people spoke I could place their approximate locations. We each placed our K2, EMF, and audio recorders on the ground in front of us.

Kat began asking questions, and shortly after her K2 lit up. She asked the spirits to move to the lights and tried to find out who they were, what happened to them, and when they died. She continued when suddenly my K2 went to red.

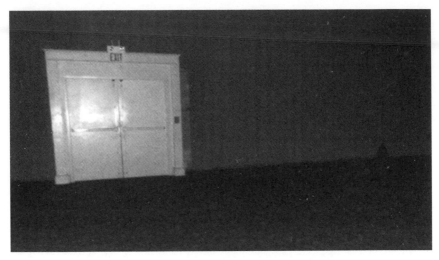

The sound stage was a large dark room.

When I spoke to the spirit, we seemed to get responses. After several questions about age, we determined he was 28. More questions revealed he was in a production of Carousel and played drums. Well, go figure. EMF was very high in certain areas near the floor, so we had to be careful when placing the meters. There are probably electrical cables running throughout the sound stage.

As we were wondering about these strange responses, Judy, Kat, and I picked up a sweet smell, like perfume. It only lasted a few seconds.

Then the four of us moved to a small room, cluttered with chairs, rugs, and a piano in the back. While there, a K2 flickered. That was followed by a soft banging noise. What was that? Questions began and Holly asked if it was a man or woman. The K2 responded to woman. She then asked the woman's age, which was between twenty and twenty-five. It appeared we had a man and woman with us, possibly actors or college students.

On another visit to the sound stage, Maria Holt-Aistrop, Kat, and I found ourselves in the large hall again. During the day it is a beautiful area with large windows looking across the expansive grounds. That night, the moon was big and bright—really illuminating the hall. The last time Kat and I were here this area seemed heavy and depressing, but not tonight.

Dawn James was with us and took Kat into the sound stage to show her the spot she had a personal experience earlier that evening.

Maria and I stayed in the hall. I began by asking the spirits to let us know they were present by lighting the K2. The meter flickered. Maria came over, and when the lights settled down we continued with questions.

We asked if it was a man and received a response. Several questions followed that went unanswered. It must have been a wave of electricity that just passed through. Kat and Dawn returned, and a man joined our group. Everyone agreed the K2s could be a little erratic in the sound stage. Yet ours was still except for those few reactions.

An extensive discussion followed about how beautiful the moon was tonight. Everything quieted for a while, then I asked Maria if she got her pizza the night before. Yup, her husband Ken went into town and brought back a pizza. Maria said it was delicious. Kat wanted the name of the pizza place. A few minutes were spent talking about pizza. Yes we were getting bored.

Then out of the corner of my eye, I saw the K2 flicker all the way to red. I asked, "Do you like pizza?" There was another emphatic response. Maria began to see what items the spirit liked on pizza. He responded positively to every item except anchovies. I said, "Nobody likes anchovies?" Kat said, "He seems to." It was a weak response and that doesn't count. Dawn wanted to know what kind of crust he liked. Maria moved into drinks with pizza. The K2 reacted to cola, but really lit up when I asked about beer. Well that settles it; this spirit is a college student since those are the two staples of dorm life.

Kat and I don't think any of us were taking this too seriously. It seemed like there were direct responses to questions, but for goodness sake, we were talking about pizza. Our minds quickly changed when Maria sent us an EVP she captured during that time. She had just asked if the spirit wanted her to eat a piece for him. A very clear male voice answers, "Make it with cheese, Maria." She has a way with ghosts.

Maria approaches the K2 while we all discuss pizza with the spirits.

That was really all we collected during that particular part of the investigation. However, our guests investigating in the sound stage had some profound experiences.

Kat and I always say if you don't capture activity on audio or camera, it didn't happen. Personal experiences aren't enough to prove the paranormal, well at least to prove it to others. So we want to talk briefly about an experience that didn't happen, because it was not recorded. A strange chain of events involved our friend Dawn James and roughly six more people in her group.

Twelve of them were in the dim soundstage hall listening to the tour guide. Eyes wandering as the guide spoke, Dawn saw movement along with about half of the group. She was startled to see the full shadow of a man walking. He was about six feet tall, stocky, and moving quickly. Dawn and the people with her were stationary.

No one moved until the shadow man walked right through the wall; that's when one of the men sprang into action. He checked the interior surroundings then ran outside to see if he could find the man that created the shadow. No luck. There wasn't a soul in the building or outside that wasn't accounted for, so the shadow man was unexplainable.

Once in the dark sound stage, Dawn thought she saw another shadow going through a door. She followed it into a back hallway. No one was there except Dawn and a man who joined her. They both had K2 meters. Standing in the darkness, Dawn was telling him what she saw and then the K2 hit. They continued talking as the K2s lit.

Were their imaginations on fire because of the earlier shadow man sighting? Maybe their high levels of energy were causing the reactions. Unexpectedly, they heard a man's voice. Seeming to come out of nowhere it was muffled and the words were lost to them.

Taken aback, their eyes darted around the small, bleak hall. Suddenly Dawn felt a tug on her hair followed by a poke in her side. Enough is enough; they quickly left the area. She had a red mark on her side that lasted for days. Dawn's next trip to Mission Point will not include an investigation of the sound stage. She is staying away.

Since no one captured the shadows or voices, it didn't happen, but we will never convince Dawn and the people with her. To them, that was one bizarre experience they will never forget.

Both the theater and sound stage carried high levels of activity each time they were visited. Todd Clements claims something is always going on at these locations.

For our weekend ghost hunts that was without question the case. Both on the island and at Mission Point Resort, evidence of the paranormal was frequent.

Who roams the grounds at the resort and why do they stay? That is something Kat and I have talked about a lot since our last visit. The answer is very simple, we simply don't know.

Mackinac Island and Mission Point Resort have expansive histories. The southeast portion of the island was considered sacred ground to the Native Americans. Mission Point Resort, over its nearly two hundred years of existence has had hundreds of thousands of guests.

Harvey may be wandering the resort, but there could be so many others. We will go back to the island and resort for answers. Chances are we will never know the ghosts of Mission Point Resort.

Photo Credits

Photographs were taken by the authors except where credited below. Images are listed in order of appearance.

Story One: Bath School Disaster
Historic Photos Courtesy of the Bath School Museum

Story Two: Lady of the Lake
Big Rapids at turn of the century.
Credit: *Big Rapids, Michigan: The water Power City* (Seely & Lowrey Publishing, 1906)

Alvin Holen
Credit: *The History and Achievements of the Fort Sheridan Officers' Training Camps* (Fort Sheridan Association)

Trenches were filled with disease, rodents and fallen soldiers.
Credit: Wikimedia Commons, Public Domain

Verdun, A major battlefield in World War I where thousands lost their lives.
Credit: *Collier's New Photographic History of the World's War* (P.F. Collier, 1919)

Pershing led troops in the bloody Second Battle of the Marne
Credit: *Chateau Thierry and the Aisne–Marne Operation 1918 US Army* (US Army film archives)

Alvin Holen lost his life during a counter offensive at Château-Thierry during the Second Battle of the Marne
Credit: Wikimedia Commons, Public Domain

Story Three: Cottonwood B&B
Randi and Andrew Roen were hardworking immigrants from Norway.
Credit: Courtesy of Cottonwood Bed & Breakfast

Original Roen family home
Credit: Courtesy of Cottonwood Bed and Breakfast

Roen boys from L to R: Alfred, Gilbert, Benhart, Sievert. Front: Andrew
Credit: Courtesy of Cottonwood Bed and Breakfast

Ben was found dead staring at the eagle
Credit: Courtesy of David Taghon, Empire Area Museum

Story Four: Hotel Montcalm

Hotel Montcalm at the turn of the century
Credit: Courtesy Hotel Montcalm Bed and Breakfast

Frank chased Amanda down this road, Main Street, and shot her.
Credit: Courtesy Hotel Montcalm Bed and Breakfast

Frank was found guilty of murdering his wife and sentenced to life in solitary confinement at the brutal Jackson State Prison.
Credit: Grand Rapids Press

Al Capone stayed at a cottage not far from here and may have conducted business over dinner at the hotel.
Credit: Wikimedia Commons, Public Domain

Did we capture gang members planning Red's demise?
Credit: Public Domain

Story Five: Sam's Joint

Long before the white man, Plainwell was home to Ottawa tribes
Credit: 19th Century engraving by Alfred Bobbet, Wikimedia Commons.

The Red Brick Inn, built by Calvin White
Credit: Courtesy of Historian Sandy Stramm

James Fennimore Cooper spent the night at The Red Brick Inn during research of his book, "Oak Openings"
Credit: Wikimedia Commons, Public Domain

Dybbuk
Credit: Wikimedia Commons, Public Domain. Art by Ephraim Moshe Lilien (1874-1925)

Story Six: Eaton County Courthouse

Charlotte Sanitarium
Credit: Courthouse Square Association

Dr. Wallace E. Newark
Credit: Courthouse Square Association

Drawing of early Sheriff's Residence shows the jailhouse extending from the back
Credit: Courthouse Square Association

Downtown Charlotte at turn of the century
Credit: Courthouse Square Association

The Phenix House and Charlotte Williams Hotel
Credit: Courthouse Square Association

The Carnegie Library where angry townsmen rallied to seek revenge on
    Copeland
Credit: Courthouse Square Association

Story Seven: Anchor Inn

This historic hotel was called Cliff's in the 1940's
Credit: Courtesy of the Anchor Inn

Marie Best with two friends.
Credit: Courtesy of Rhonda Spears at the Anchor Inn

Dark shadow seen on the second floor
Credit: Drawn by Miranda Spears, courtesy of Ronda Spears

Second shadow seen
Credit: Drawn by Miranda Spears, courtesy of Ronda Spears

Miranda's scratches
Credit: Courtesy of Ronda Spears at the Anchor Inn

North American ley lines
Credit: Courtesy of: Peter Champoux, author of Gaia Matrix, www.
    geometryofplace.com

Two major ley lines, First Nation and Kachina, intersect in Houghton Lake.
Credit: Courtesy of: Peter Champoux, author of Gaia Matrix, www.
    geometryofplace.com

Story Eight: Carriage House

The Carriage House Circa 1865
Credit: Courtesy of Carriage House Bed and Breakfast

Story Nine: Mackinac Island Introduction

All photos by the authors.

Story Ten: Fort Holmes

Fort Holmes showing the old observation tower
Credit: Wikimedia Commons, "Old Fort Holmes, from Robert N. Dennis
    collection of stereoscopic views"

Story Fourteen: Mission Point Introduction

Mission Point Church is one of the oldest in the Midwest
Credit: Wikimedia Commons, Public Domain

About the Authors

Kathleen Tedsen and Beverlee Rydel

Kat and Bev continue their search into the world of the paranormal with their third book, *Haunted Travels of Michigan III: SPIRITS RISING*. This follows the success of their previous two releases.

Book one received the *International Paranormal Acknowledgement Award for Best Paranormal/Educational Book and Authors*. A story from book two was selected and adapted for the SyFy Network television series *Paranormal Witness* episode "Lady on the Stairs."

Over the years Kat and Bev have been guest speakers at major Michigan and Midwest paranormal conferences featuring some of the biggest names in the paranormal community, including members of SyFy Ghost Hunters, Ghost Hunters International, John Zaffis and his Haunted Collector crew, Stanton Friedman, and many others.

Kat and Bev are especially proud of their work with Pure Michigan. Over the past few years they have conducted live, on-line chats and blogs for Michigan's official travel and tourism site. They are always happy to answer and share stories about some of their favorite Michigan haunts.

Kat and Bev are not new to writing. In 1991 they authored their first book series, *Michigan Vacation Guide*. It was placed on the Secretary of State's "Read Michigan" list in 1995.

With their paranormal book series, the authors approach each investigation with a skeptic's eye. To Bev and Kat, investigations are not just about hauntings but about the history of the location and lives of the people that may have created the haunting. They will spend months of historical research on each story. If they can connect true historical events and people to evidence, it may get them get closer to understanding what creates a haunting.

The authors want to share their experiences with the reader and take them into the ghost hunt. To accomplish this, each story contains a password that allows access to Secret Rooms on their website. In the Secret Room, readers can see photographs as well as video and audio of evidence collected during the investigation.

The authors began their paranormal journey as skeptics. Today, they know that in many cases there is something out there that cannot be explained. Something paranormal.

They continue their search into the unknown in this third book of their Haunted Travels of Michigan series.